KEEP FIGHTING, STOP STRUGGLING

THE MILES LEVIN STORY

D1259082

KEEP FIGHTING,
STOP STRUGGLING

THE MILES LEVIN STORY

A Work in Nonfiction

BY

MILES ALPERN LEVIN (Deceased)

Commentary by: Jonathan E. Levin (yoni11@comcast.net)

Edited by Dianne Rice (drice0209@aol.com)

Cover Illustration: Ellen Rutt

Cover Photography: Titan Professional Photo Lab, Troy, MI

Back Cover Photography: Self portrait by Miles Levin

Website: www.levinstory.com

www.bookstandpublishing.com

Published by
Bookstand Publishing
Morgan Hill, CA 95037
3434_3

ISBN 978-1-61863-004-9

Printed in the United States of America

Dedicated to all kids with cancer —

for your courage, suffering, hope,

and trust.

FOREWORD

By Bob Woodruff

Meeting and getting to spend time with Miles Levin was a life changer for me as it was for thousands of others all over the world. Less than a year before he died of alveolar rhabdomyosarcoma cancer I happened to meet him and his parents passing through the Detroit airport's security line. He was only 18 years old, but he knew that he would not live much longer.

Perhaps there was a reason I got the chance to know Miles. He was about to graduate from Cranbrook School, the same high school I left 28 years earlier. He was being treated in the Beaumont Hospital of Royal Oak, the same hospital where I was born in 1961. And Miles was just a few years older than my own son Mack, who was a sophomore in high school.

I had suffered a change in life myself just a year before I met Miles. I was nearly killed by an explosive device triggered by an insurgent in Iraq in 2006. While I survived I understood what it meant to change priorities, to see the preciousness of life by something that is thrust on you, and to accept the reality of what happens.

What Miles did with the time he had left was nothing less than extraordinary. He directed himself onto a different path than most of his friends, and he set out to make people aware not only of his disease but of the process of dying with dignity. He talked, he blogged, and while his friends were heading off to colleges and careers that would launch them into life, he inspired us with emotion and insights; with lessons and smiles. I want to share with you just some of the thoughts and writings he composed that touched me. They were so incredibly advanced for a high school student and personally I had never read anything quite like this:

"Dying is not what scares me; it's dying having had no impact. I know a lot of eyes are watching me suffer; and — win or lose — this is my time for impact."

Miles made gigantic impact. He launched his website on an adventure that brought him to people in the States, Europe and Asia. His fellow students wore t-shirts with the slogan "keep fighting, stop struggling." His story found its way from the front pages of newspapers to national TV.

I am so lucky to have become friends with Miles and his family Nina, Nancy and Jon. I had the honor of sharing the stage with Miles for his high school commencement speech in 2007. I had stood in this same spot as a graduate in 1979. This time Miles silenced the crowd. His mother Nancy summed this up after he died, not just about his words, but also about his love for living.

"Miles went from a boy-man to a man-boy. At a cost that would knock your socks off, Miles still managed to pack a wallop. He could not and would not be held back ... from living life to the fullest."

Miles Levin is one of the most remarkable people I ever met. He died just 6 days before his 19th birthday, just a few hours before I turned 46. He taught us all this: The quality of life does not depend only on your number of years on this earth. It is the depth of your love and the width of your inspiration.

TABLE OF CONTENTS

Tired
And lonely,
So tired
The heart aches.
Meltwater trickles
Down the rocks,
The fingers are numb,
The knees tremble.
It is now,
Now, that you must not give in.

On the path of the others
Are resting places,
Places in the sun
Where they can meet.
But this
Is your path,
And it is now,
Now, that you must not fail.

Weep
If you can,
Weep,
But do not complain.
The way chose you -
And you must be thankful.

Dag Hammarskjold
July 6,

From MARKINGS by Dag Hammarskjold, translated by W.H. Auden & Leif Sjoberg, translation copyright 1964, copyright renewed 1992 by Alfred A. Knopf, a division of Random House, Inc. and Faber & Faber Ltd. Used by permission of Alfred A. Knopf, a division of Random House, Inc.

INTRODUCTION

"I've been following your CarePage since the CNN story ... I need to let you know that you have touched my life and become a friend to me ... I will take your story, your legacy, wherever I go in my life and share it with the people around me ..."

- Comment at Miles' blog

This book is offered as a tribute to Miles Levin by me, his father. After an epic twenty-six month struggle for life, Miles succumbed to rhabdomyosarcoma, a soft tissue cancer. He speaks for himself in these pages through excerpts from his CarePage blog – which brought him worldwide attention.

Incongruous as it seems, his story is a success story. It is a story of triumph, not grief. It's a story about meeting challenges and finding gratitude. Miles triumphed over the fear of cancer and the fear of death. I am assured – by many of the tens of thousands who followed his updates on his blog – that knowing his story can help you in your life.

CNN acknowledged the importance of his story by following it both on its television broadcast, "Anderson Cooper 360°", and its companion website. Anderson Cooper said, "Miles Levin was a friend of mine." Newspapers and blog-sites around the world found Miles' story important. This validation assures me that reading his insightful words will help you in your own life's journey.

Bob Woodruff, renowned ABC News journalist, said of Miles, "... he has told us what it means to live life without fear, but with joy."

Miles Levin gained wide recognition and praise by eloquently sharing his deepest thoughts and feelings while adjusting to his new identity as a cancer patient. He is extraordinarily honest and forthright. The transition from boyhood to manhood is made visible through his writing. I feel confident that his remarkable words have the power to benefit anyone who reads them.

This book begins with a frightened teenager. It lets the reader see into the inner recesses of his mind and heart where he makes a series of decisions that lead him to look squarely at death – and to tell what he sees with keen clarity and disarming honesty. Miles began writing on a hospital website called "CarePages." Stretching the boundaries of the site's purpose, he invested it with his spirit, making it into a destination for tens of thousands of supporters.

This book is not about death, but about a race to manhood. It's about accomplishment, intentionality, resolve, comportment and courage. While cancer was bringing an early *end* to his life, Miles made the choice to bring *completion* to his life. It is a poignant story about personal evolution, an important story about triumph over fear.

For whom is this book written, and how will it benefit them?

It's written as an inspiration for the twenty-eight million people living with some form of cancer.

It's written as a source of courage for the seven million people who will die of cancer this year.

It's written for teenagers and others with terminal diseases; it can help them to understand, cope with, confront, and use the menace they face.

It's written for the families of children dealing with pediatric cancer or other life-threatening diseases; it can enhance their ability to engage in their loved one's battle for survival and, if need be, prepare for their loss.

It's written for medical caregivers of all types; it can strengthen their resolve to be of true service.

It's written for psychologists, the clergy, philosophers, and students of death and dying; it can deepen their understanding of the human spirit.

It's written for those who wish to sense life's preciousness more deeply, and for anyone who wants to feel more gratitude and thus be truly alive within his or her allotted moments.

It's written for those who appreciate the English language affectively applied to profound purposes.

CHAPTER ONE

SOME BACKGROUND

Miles spent the first six years of his life in a pleasant, safe, family-oriented neighborhood on the west side of Omaha, Nebraska. His mother, Nancy, and I had moved to Omaha from Detroit, Michigan in 1986 to join the Mutual of Omaha companies as managers. Miles was born there in August of 1988, as was our daughter, Nina, in December of 1990. In 1994 we returned to Detroit where Nancy was a licensed psychologist and where I would start a property management business. Miles was about to turn seven and was ready to enter first grade. We intentionally located our house less than a mile from the Oakland Steiner School, a private primary school based on the Waldorf educational model.

What Miles learned of classical mythology and heroism at this school would later be a source of courage for him. The overarching goal of a Waldorf education is to provide its students with the basis on which to develop into free, moral and integrated individuals – and to help every child fulfill his or her unique destiny. I feel this last to be an important part of what Miles received from his Waldorf education.

Miles graduated from the Waldorf School in June, 2002. In September, 2003, Miles began ninth grade as a fifteen-year-old newcomer to the upper school of Cranbrook Kingswood Academy, a private school a few miles from our house. Cranbrook Kingswood, established in 1928 by newspaper publisher George Booth and his wife Ellen Scripps Booth, continues to be a highly respected institution. It is part of a rolling, verdant campus which includes a scientific institute, a successful artistic community, exceptional architecture, and kindergarten through twelfth grade co-ed education. The student body is comprised of both those who are boarders from around the world and day students and day students from the surrounding communities.

Cranbrook Kingswood is an expensive school for those who don't have scholarships. The cost was, in fact, beyond our reach. But the tuition was a gift from Miles' maternal grandparents, who had set funds aside for the education of their eight grandchildren.

Because most of his classmates had attended Cranbrook Kingswood from an early age Miles faced the challenge of being a newcomer. It did not help, particularly in Detroit where cars are essential status symbols, our car was a relative "beater".

Miles was savvy enough not to be too eager to make strides socially. In his own slow, winning way he began to make friends. He went out for football and became respected for his understanding of the game and his intense drive to play well. He took a variety of classes and gradually became acquainted with his classmates. It wasn't long before some of these new friends, boys and girls, began showing up at our house.

Miles was not one to overcompensate with displays of bravado or brashness to make an impression. He had the steady, gentle warmth of a simmering crock pot and a wry, witty sense of humor. He was a soft spoken, natural gentleman with a thick mane of auburn hair. Strong, supple and well-proportioned, he had wide shoulders and a narrow waist. It wasn't long before the girls took notice of him and gave him their stamp of approval, which influenced the attitude of the boys. During Miles' first year at Cranbrook he made many friends and was accepted into numerous social circles.

Miles had the world by the tail. He had great prospects, having been born in a country of endless opportunity and raised in an unbroken, secure and happy family by devoted parents. He had a secular and moral education of high quality. He was a good looking, well-adjusted teenager. Many kids his age would probably have felt envious of his circumstances, his advantages, and his life were it not for the severe turn it took during the first week of June, 2005.

CHAPTER TWO

ONSET

In June of 2005, Miles had just completed the tenth grade, his second year at Cranbrook Kingswood. It was a good year, full of academic, athletic, and social accomplishments. He acquired his driver's license and my Honda for his use. Because of the increased risk of accidents among young drivers, I enrolled Miles and myself in a father-son defensive driving course on tour in the United States. It was scheduled for 1:00 p.m. on Saturday, June 4, 2005, at the Silverdome stadium's large parking lot, only two miles from our house.

The day was pleasant and warm, so I asked Miles to mow the lawn prior to our leaving for the driving course. At about 10:00 a.m., Miles put on some earphones to listen to music on his iPod, started the mower, and went at it. From inside the house I could hear the mower making its passes. But after a half-hour, the sound of the motor stopped and Miles came into the house, limping and clutching his abdomen. He sat down at the kitchen counter, resting his head on his arms. I thought perhaps he'd injured himself, but he said he had a stabbing pain in his lower right abdomen. I immediately suspected an inflamed appendix.

I asked my wife to join us and I told her what I suspected. Since we were planning to leave on vacation the following Saturday, Nancy thought Miles should be taken to the closest Emergency Room for an evaluation. We didn't want to be a thousand miles from home and have our son need an emergency appendectomy. Miles' pain had subsided by the time he and I got into my Toyota Prius. Because there was concern, but no longer a sense of panic, we swung by the Silverdome on the way to the hospital to let them know that we wouldn't be participating. We then drove another two miles to St. Joseph Hospital, parked, and walked inside.

Our health insurance coverage came to us through my second job with Oakland University, a local public university where I was part of the operations staff for its historic properties. Although no one in the family had a history of serious health incidents or concerns, given the hazards of being without health insurance, the insurance coverage was more important than the paycheck. This was the primary reason I'd taken the job, as my property management business provided no insurance coverage.

I showed the clerk my insurance card and we were quickly processed and directed to the ER waiting room. Miles was in less pain and I was less concerned. After a short wait, a nurse took us to an examining room; we were soon visited by the attending physician who did a brief examination. He agreed it could be anything from constipation to appendicitis, but he advised us that a scan - which would take about ninety minutes - should be performed. Would we have declined this scan if we'd had no insurance coverage?

The results showed a troubling area of contrast in the prostate region, and some involvement of the lymph nodes there. The doctor recommended that Miles' pediatrician be alerted immediately and that a follow-up be arranged. His opinion and findings were very sobering. Our attention was suddenly focused on the gravity of the situation. A routine appendicitis was no longer our concern.

Over the remainder of the weekend we contacted friends and relatives who worked in the medical field. My father and brother, and Nancy's uncle and brother, were physicians, so we had many medical contacts. Their advice was simply to gather more diagnostic information. Through Miles' pediatrician, we arranged a consultation. The meeting was scheduled for the following Monday in Royal Oak at Beaumont Hospital. Beaumont Health System is a highly respected institution with numerous satellite facilities and affiliated clinics. Its first, and largest, campus had been located in the city of Royal Oak since 1950.

The examination on Monday resulted in a prescription for pain medication to be taken as needed, and an order for two procedures: a bladder scoping and a prostate biopsy. These were scheduled for the following Thursday. Miles hadn't experienced a recurrence of the acute pain he'd had while mowing the lawn. With the subsidence of symptoms, we took up the question of whether to cancel our scheduled vacation. We asked the physicians if they had any concerns about our leaving; they saw no reason to cancel the trip as the biopsy results would take a few days. Our decision was influenced by two issues beyond the doctors' reassurances. We had arranged to have our home's hardwood floors sanded and refinished while we were away, making the living space uninhabitable. Also, we hadn't taken out trip-cancellation insurance. All things considered, we decided to continue with our vacation plans. This proved to be a fateful decision.

On Saturday we boarded a flight to Savannah, Georgia. On the plane Miles began to feel some abdominal pain, but he considered it manageable. In Savannah, we rented a car and started driving to Brunswick where, on Sunday morning, we were to take a ferryboat to the resort on Cumberland Island. But on Saturday afternoon, while driving from Savannah to Brunswick, Miles' abdominal pain became much worse. Nancy and I looked at each other with sudden concern about the wisdom of having left Detroit on this sojourn. We decided it would be foolish to be on an island off the coast of Georgia with our son in precarious health. We agreed to abort the trip and get back to Detroit as soon as possible. But it was already dusk and we were road weary, and numerous calls needed to be made to arrange our return trip. It seemed sensible to stay in a motel for one night and return to Detroit the following morning.

We found a motel room in Brunswick. Nancy, who is very adept at travel arrangements, started calling airlines and car rental agents to notify them of our change of plans. She also called the physicians to let them know we'd be returning on Sunday. Just as these calls were being made, Miles pain became extreme. It was unbearable if he tried to stand erect, so he walked like a hunchback. We managed to get a prescription for Vicodin with Codeine and found a pharmacy to provide it.

One conversation Nancy had that night was with urologist, Ken Kernan. Dr. Kernan told Nancy he had received the results of the analysis of the prostate tissue taken by biopsy the previous Thursday. He said it had proven to be cancerous – in words she'll never forget, "It's Rhabdo." There was some further cell-typing and staging to be done, but we now learned Miles was in big trouble. Rhabdomyosarcoma is a rare, soft tissue cancer which occurs in the muscles or organs of young children and adolescents. Its cause and genetic origins aren't well understood. Medical science is not currently able to predict its occurrence. It can be found attached to muscle tissue, wrapped around intestines, or in any anatomic location. Most cases occur in areas naturally lacking in skeletal muscle, such as the head, neck, and genitourinary tract. In the United States there are only about 300 cases per year of alveolar rhabdomyosarcoma, the type Miles was later determined to have. If found and removed before it metastasizes, survival rates are approximately seventy percent. After metastasis, we were told, four out of five alveolar rhabdo patients die within five years.

By Sunday evening we'd managed to return to Detroit with our son in acute pain. By prior arrangement, we took him directly to the pediatric wing of Beaumont Hospital in Royal Oak, where he became a patient of Dr. Charles Main, an oncologist with over thirty years experience. The trial had begun.

CHAPTER THREE

A NEW DIMENSION

Having admitted Miles as an inpatient to Beaumont Hospital, his mother, sister Nina and I found accommodations away from our home while our wood floors were being refinished. Nancy stayed with Miles in his hospital room. Nina stayed at the home of a classmate. I stayed at my mother's house in Birmingham, just one and a half miles from the hospital.

The reasons for Miles' admission were 1) to handle his pain crisis; 2) to stage, or classify, his cancer; and 3) to initiate chemotherapy. For the pain crisis, morphine was given as needed. The cancer staging was explained to us by Dr. Main and his assistant, Norma, in a treatment meeting on Friday, June 17. Staging was based upon criteria established by the Children's Oncology Group (COG) of the National Cancer Institute. It placed Miles' cancer in Stage 3, meaning that the cancer had advanced into his lymph nodes below the level of the renal arteries, those supplying the kidneys with blood. The administration of chemotherapy was set for Wednesday, June 22, and would be based on a protocol using three anti-cancer agents: Vincristine, Actinomycin D, and Cyclophosphamide. In order to administer the chemotherapeutic agents, a doctor placed a Bard Port in Miles' left chest wall. This port delivered the drugs directly into the superior vena cava, a large vein, rather than through smaller diameter veins which could be damaged by the caustic drugs. An experienced surgeon, Dr. Morden, implanted the mediport on Monday, June 20. While Miles was sedated and anesthetized for the Bard Port placement, other surgeons, Doctors Kernen and Bennett, hoped to address problems Miles had with urination. Thus began the first of many medical and surgical treatments and procedures done in an effort to preserve a life.

While waiting for Miles to come out of surgery, I noticed, in the lobby area of the pediatric floor, a kiosk that had a keyboard, monitor and track ball. I thought it might be an arcade game for the kids. A closer look showed that it was a dedicated station for accessing a single website: www.CarePages.com. I read the orientation material and saw that CarePages was an online community of people coming together to share the challenges, hopes and triumphs of patients facing a life-changing health event. CarePages helps members and their families connect during and after hospitalization for illnesses ranging from cancer, spinal cord injury, stroke, heart disease to premature birth. It is also a place for patients with chronic conditions to journal about their experience or connect with others facing similar circumstances.

Through personalized Care Pages, members relate their stories, posted photos and updated friends and family instantly. In turn, friends and family of patients send messages of love and encouragement. The website also provides discussion forums, blogs, and articles to educate and guide members through their health journey. The CarePages mission statement reads: To ensure that no one goes through a health challenge alone.

Eric and Sharon Langshur founded CarePages in 2000 after their son, Matthew, was born with a heart defect. Eric and Sharon struggled to find a way to keep in touch with family and friends about Matthew's condition. Sharon's brother set up the first CarePages patient website to help. Today, Matthew Langshur is a healthy kid, and CarePages has grown to reach millions of families across the globe.

We had already been besieged by phone calls from family and friends wanting to know about Miles' situation. I saw that the the CarePage website could be a convenient clearinghouse for those who were concerned. Without hesitation, using the instructions provided at the kiosk, I created a CarePage for Miles, naming it "LevinMiles." Later that day, I sent out a notice by e-mail telling friends and family that they could obtain updates about Miles and leave messages for him at the LevinMiles CarePage. I also wrote the first CarePage update so that people would find some content when they registered themselves as readers of the LevinMiles CarePage.

On Tuesday June 21, 2005 I came to understand that we had entered a new dimension and left another behind, perhaps irretrievably. In the previous treatment meeting, we had been told that the chemo agents prescribed for Miles might compromise the viability of his sperm. He might, in fact, be rendered sterile. We were advised to arrange to have a specimen of Miles' sperm placed into a cryogenic sperm bank. We were given a referral to a nearby physician's office which maintained a sperm bank. Taking the referral information into my hand had a chilling effect. It made everything so real. It was consequences time. I took the contact information and called to make an appointment for the following day.

The next morning Miles received a temporary discharge pass from the hospital and I took him to the sperm bank, on the second floor of a building immediately across from a luxury hotel. After registration Miles took a specimen container to a room and was told to take his time. While waiting for Miles, I stood at a window which overlooked the hotel entry across the street and saw about twenty youngsters, mostly boys in their early teens, holding basketballs and waiting in line along the sidewalk. The receptionist told me that a professional basketball team was staying at the hotel and the kids were hoping to snag autographs from the players. Looking at the excited young people, I felt as if I were looking through a lens into another dimension, the one which we had previously inhabited. I thought, "Such simplicity and innocence is no longer ours. Those days are gone, forever."

Wednesday, Miles' experienced his chemotherapy. He was registered to Children's Oncology Group (COG) Protocol D9803, and randomized to Regimen A. The randomization meant "we don't know what works." He received a three-drug combination and left for home on Thursday evening, June 23, having been in the hospital for eleven days. On Friday afternoon, after learning from me about the creation of his CarePage, he wasted no time going there to read the messages that had accumulated. They were all from extended family – aunts, uncles, cousins – saying things like "We're pulling for you……you're a soldier….you can definitely beat this….don't pinch the nurses," etc. Then Miles wrote his first update:

I'll write something more substantial when I am feeling better, but I've just read all the messages and wanted to thank you for all your love and support. A lot of the time I feel pretty unconfident about these upcoming 42 weeks of chemo, so this is just what I need. Thank you all. Miles

Brief as it was, Miles' update affirmed that the CarePage readers' comments helped him. The responses to his first update were much meatier, asking for more detail about his disease and its treatment, telling of their own direct or indirect brushes with cancer, telling of the establishment of prayer circles on Miles' behalf, and sending continued hugs and love. Messages began coming from more remote relatives as news of Miles' situation reached them.

On June 27, Miles posted a brief update:

> "To my dismay, sugar makes tumors grow like crazy. It cant be vegatables or vitamins that are bad, it has to be sugar!"

On June 28, his first message from outside the family arrived. Karen Melaas, a congregant at our temple, whose children had also attended Cranbrook, began her long tenure as a LevinMiles CarePage visitor by typing a message of encouragement. She also sent Miles a pair of boxing gloves as emblematic of his fight for life.

Miles began to use the CarePage to sort out his growing understanding of the disease and its treatment, describing what went on in his weekly appointments and the meaning of some of the lab values. He reported on side effects of his treatment and talked about his social activities. But then, on July 4, and again on July 7, he wrote updates that marked the beginning of his use of the CarePage to reveal and share deeper, more soulful ruminations, ruminations that reflected a change in character, and that struck a new chord with his readers. The one on July 4 merely said, in its entirety, "My hair is starting to fall out. I'm finding it very distressing." But the next update represented a real leap. It has since been published in articles and books, and is still circulating in cyberspace:

> "I went to the driving range the other day and I was thinking....
>
> I was thinking how you start out with a big bucket of golf balls, and you just start hitting away carelessly. You have dozens of them, each individual ball means nothing so you just hit, hit, hit. One ball gone is practically inconsequential when subtracted from your bottomless bucket. There are no practice swings or technique re-evaluations after a bad shot, because so many tries remain. Yet eventually you have to reach down towards the bottom of the bucket to scavenge for another shot and you realize that tries are running out. Now with just a handful left, each swing becomes more

meaningful. The right technique becomes more crucial, so between each shot you take a couple practice swings and a few deep breaths. There is a very strong need to end on a good note, even if every preceding shot was horrible, *getting it right at the end means a lot.* You know as you tee up your last ball, 'this is my final shot, I want to crush this with perfection; I must make this count.' Limited quantities or limited time brings a new, precious value and significance to anything you do. Live every day shooting as if it's your last shot. I know I have to. I found out today 5 year survival rates are just 30%."

CarePage readers detected a shift in focus on Miles' part from the physical to the spiritual that made an impression. As he deepened his updates, revealing more of his inner state, his readers revealed more of themselves in their comments. And the circle of readers, which already consisted of many friends, widened to include even more distant relatives, and people we knew from previous phases of life: friends from Omaha, Miles' classmates and teachers from primary school, colleagues of mine from the past, people from my group bicycle rides, and so on.

Meanwhile, Miles' mother discovered the value of the internet, especially the search function of Google. Nancy began wending and winding her way across and through the internet, identifying "centers of excellence" in cancer treatment, finding the names of key Rhabdomyosarcoma researchers, learning about the relative efficacy of various drugs, and discovering Rhabdo related organizations, foundations, clinical trials, and study groups. Through this effort she identified Carola S. Arndt as one of the world's leading rhabdo experts and decided to seek a second opinion from her. Dr. Arndt was study chair of the Children's Oncology Group clinical trials and chief pediatric oncologist at the Mayo Clinic. Dr Arndt is consulted on approximately one in six of the 300 cases of Rhabdo diagnosed in the United States each year.

Learning of rhabdomyosarcoma's terrible virulence, Nancy wanted Dr. Arndt's recommendation for the most aggressive course of treatment; Nancy wanted removal of the cancer tissue by surgery; she wanted more sensitive imaging protocols, like positron-emission tomography (PET) scans and the use of cutting-edge chemotherapeutic drugs, like Topotecan. And she wanted to know if relapse was as dismal an indicator as she had read.

Dr. Arndt read Miles' medical history, reviewed the previous charts and scans, and did her own physical examination of Miles. She then created a clinical report which endorsed none of Nancy's wishes. Dr. Arndt suggested that surgery could do nothing that radiation couldn't. She said that PET imaging was not the standard of care and that it was more important to pick one form of imaging, either MRI or CT, and stick with it. Dr. Arndt said that no drug regimen had a better track record with Rhabdo than VAC (the Vincristine, Actinomycin D, and Cyclophosphamide combination). She told Nancy Topotecan was too new to have a track record. And she indicated that relapse is rarely survived. Finally, to ice the cake, Dr. Arndt delivered the news that Miles' cancer was Stage 4, not Stage 3. She made this determination by jointly reviewing previous scans with a Mayo Clinic radiologist, and finding evidence of cancer in the lymph nodes above the level of the renal arteries. She concluded her report by saying that she would not recommend any changes in drugs or treatment protocol, and that "surgery would not add to his outcome." Was she saying that he was going to die no matter what?

Dr. Arndt found that the cancer was more extensive than had previously been determined. At this point in the disease, the different findings didn't change the treatment recommendations. But there may have been opportunities earlier in the course of the disease which might have led to a timelier discovery of the cancer.

When Miles went for a routine annual check-up early in 2005, he told the doctor about abdominal pain, or in so many words, a stomachache. Looking at an otherwise healthy sixteen-year-old with no history of prior disease, hearing a vague complaint about a tummy ache, what was the doctor to do? But had the doctor been able to turn to more sensitive diagnostic resources, would he have discovered the cancer at that point? If so, would the cancer have been limited to a single location at that time? According to research literature, patients with *localized* Rhabdomyosarcoma have cure rates of 60% to 75% with surgery, radiation and adjuvant chemotherapy. In contrast, once metastasized, cure rates plummet to 20%, and decline to near zero after relapse.

(www.liddyshriversarcomainitiative.org/Newsletters/V02N04/AP23 573/ap23573.htm).

An article by Thomas Goetz in the January, 2008 issue of "Wired Magazine," posits that early detection is the best way to beat cancer. He suggests that our cure-driven, late-stage approach has yielded meager results. Overall cancer mortality rates have declined by 8% since 1975, whereas heart disease deaths have decreased by nearly 60% in the same period. Early detection is an afterthought in cancer research. The National Cancer Institute spends only eight percent of its total budget on detection and diagnosis research.

Our chief concern now was not how he acquired cancer, but how to get rid of it; and in the meantime how to live with it. In July, 2005, Miles was about six weeks out from the beginning of his eleventh grade of high school. Nancy was of the opinion that Miles should not enroll in classes. She thought that the chemo, radiation, and possibly surgery would be the cause of too many absences. She practically demanded that he take a year off from school. This caused him to make the following update on July 26, 2005:

July 26, 2005 at 06:21 PM EDT

A solar eclipse.

As far as I can remember, this will be my first update posted in a very frustrated mood. I am thoroughly and stubbornly determined to go back to school this year. I will gladly accept any modifications or outside tutors or whatever I need to do. I am feeling way to (sic) strong to sit around for an entire year. Most days I feel basically the way I did a year ago. I had chemo this morning, and I feel fine. I might just be angry, and just as pain does to lesser pains, it pushes the sickness to the background. For me to sit around at home each and every day of the fall, winter, and spring would be both needlessly unproductive and highly depressing. What's the problem, then?... Admittedly a little irrational, but there is something about The First Day back at school that I want to be there for. ...It's a lot. I'm more worried about the surgery itself but I don't even want to get into that right now.

Miles was presenting a logistical problem in real time to his readers and they responded in force. While trying to be empathetic, most of the "grownups" suggested he accept the compromise of missing some school. Denise McCauley, a local actress wrote, "Any actor will tell you that an entrance late in the script can be a good thing." Her husband, Jim, wrote, "I believe healing is more important now and so be it if that is best for you in the long run." Miles' Uncle Harlan wrote, "Your primary job over the next year is to support your body mentally and physically to be cured of this cancer." My cousin Glenn Cantor, a pharmaceutical researcher, said, "Schools are places that teem with infectious diseases. You will need to stay home whenever your white counts are low."

All of this advice influenced Miles as reflected in his July 31, 2005 update. "I am trying to own up to any denial I have about the normality (or lack of normality) in my new life." But he also chided the adults for their eagerness to proffer advice, making reference to Mark Twain's remark that "Few things are harder to put up with than the annoyance of a good example."

Miles' life began to oscillate between extremes, and his updates reflected this. On August 4, he reported his great pleasure in the results of scans that indicated significant tumor shrinkage. This confirmed that the chemo was at least having an effect and, to the delight of his readers, that we were moving in the right direction. Then, following administration of Vincristine, Miles had thirty-six hours of profound nausea and vomiting. He had not previously had such a negative reaction to Vincristine alone, and he feared that if his drug sensitivity continued to increase, his plan to go back to school in September was in jeopardy.

But on August 13, after extensive discussion between members of our family, the medical team, and the deans and faculty of Cranbrook, it was decided that Miles would be allowed to return to school. Whatever accommodations were necessary would be devised. Miles wrote, "I am very grateful."

Miles continued to pick up new readers. David Carlson, my college roommate from thirty-five years previous, got wind of the situation. He wrote to Miles about his own struggles with cancer. Another cancer survivor, Jonny Immerman, came to the CarePages by way of mutual friends. Jonny, in his early thirties, had recently started a non-profit organization based in Chicago which teamed up new pediatric cancer patients with survivors of cancer. The organization was called Immerman's Angels. Jonny decided to pair himself with Miles. Jonny, a testicular cancer survivor and a Cranbrook grad, had a unique, upbeat way of expressing himself. He called Miles "buddy" and wrote with great encouragement:" Hey buddy, you sounded great in your last update…I know how hard it is to go through all of these tests, especially when you travel out of state like that...stay strong...thinking about you and sending good vibes, strength, and love from a guy who shared and still shares your shoes...I'm always here to talk...keep that chin up buddy...stay strong my man...Jonny"

On August 10, two weeks prior to Miles' 17th birthday, his uncle Wayne posted something to the CarePage that he had been working on for weeks:

"Miles, OK, man, here's something to look forward to beside chemo: you and I are going to the Red Sox vs. Detroit Tigers game in Detroit on August 17, and we have permission from both organizations to meet the World Champion Red Sox players before the game. Now that's cool! We have great seats right behind the visiting dugout. "

Wayne had been instructed to report with Miles to an intern named Walsh at Comerica Park, to the Guest Services Office, one hour prior to game time. They had been told Walsh would take them to a Vice President of Public Relations for the Boston Red Sox. But when they arrived at Guest Services, things fell apart. Walsh told them the VP had been called into an emergency meeting and that it would not be possible to go to the visiting team's locker room. As Miles tells it:

To a New Yorker with a law degree, Wayne Alpern, this would not stand. Despite being forbid by Walsh, Wayne went over to the (Boston) dugout and got the manager, Terry Francona. We started talking to him and explained my situation, and he got someone to lead us back into the club house. We went through the dugout and left the normal world behind as we walked down a hall teeming with a bunch of giant men whom I'd only seen on TV.

Throughout our quest, Walsh the Intern seemed to be intent on forbidding us from seeing anyone. He told us to wait outside the locker room and he would try and grab one of them on their way out, but could not make any promises. Kevin Millar (a player) emerged, and I went up to him and shook his hand and explained myself. He let us right in to the innermost chambers, the players' dwellings.Suddenly I found myself amidst Jonny Damon, Manny Ramirez, David Ortiz, and others. Before I could grasp this I found Damon shaking my hand and a picture of myself getting taken with him by my equally overcome uncle. I did not get tongue-tied with any of the other players or coaches, but Damon had a radiating aura to him. Photos do not do justice to this aura though, he was larger than life. Handshakes with David Ortiz, and then an autograph from Manny, then somehow we were being ushered to an elevator. It went up a couple floors and ejected us back into the regular world of oblivious fans buying hot dogs and baseballs. It was a peak moment in the lives of my uncle and me, and it would not have been possible without the determination of Wayne or the heart shown by Terry Francona."

There was something about this whole episode which suggested to me that Miles was being prepared for a special path as a cancer patient. Permission obtained to visit with a team that had achieved world-champion status against all odds, followed by the occurrence of an obstacle; the overcoming of that obstacle through persistence and readiness to act. Then admission to the inner sanctum; the acceptance and welcome by a hero figure; and the visualization of an aura. Two nights before they went to the game, Wayne had seen something too, and reported this on CarePages:

"I just flew in from New York and had a big dinner with Miles and his family. In a few days, we will meet the Red Sox. I hereby file this observer's report with the larger Miles Levin community:

Miles, in a nutshell, has become magnetic. He is striking to look at and listen to. More than ever he has become the center of attention, brimming with a constant stream of interesting insights, observations, jokes, and energy. He is undergoing a remarkable transformation: mature, open, confident, sensitive, entertaining, and I daresay, brilliant. He's sharp as a tack, very witty, and full of random interesting comments like the beauty of hamburgers being their complete lack of resemblance to a cow..... Something that's happened inside may be wrong, but whatever Miles is doing is very, very right. If his body is ailing, his mind is more than compensating. He shows no sign of embarrassment, self-consciousness, or discouragement. Miles has a glow about him. In fact, to me, he doesn't seem sick at all, but one of the healthiest people I know. All of us, in a very wide and expanding spiral, are witnessing something quite extraordinary, with Miles at the center."

The Tigers vs. Red Sox game was followed a week later by a small celebration of Miles' seventeenth birthday on August 25. He celebrated it with cousins from Boston who'd come through Detroit on their way to our family cottage in northern Michigan. Miles had not been planning to go to the cottage with them, but when his next round of chemo was postponed because of his low blood counts, Miles joined his cousins up north for a few days of sun and fun.

His next round of VAC chemotherapy took place back at home during the onslaught of hurricane Katrina in Louisiana. Miles spent a good deal of time watching the hurricane coverage on TV, including President Bush's inadequate response. Despite Miles' discomfort and nausea, he stated in an update on September 3 that his situation "could be a lot worse. It puts things in perspective to know that no matter how bad you think you've got it, if you live in America, have eaten in the last day, and make over five dollars per hour, most people on this planet would say you've got it made."

Being housebound by nausea, and spending so much time watching television, Miles was really primed to return to his schooling at Cranbrook. On September 7, his update stated, "The fact that I'm returning to school has been on my mind in the past few days, and a source of good spirits. What would I do at home all year? Sit on my couch, watch daytime TV, and feel sorry for myself. I feel sorry for anyone who has to watch daytime television all day."

Registration for school was not easy because Miles was feeling sick, vomiting frequently, and losing weight, leading to hospitalization for two days of observation. But his stoic determination was evident in his update of September 14:

It's been a week since the last posting and a lot has happened in between them. Last you read, I had just come back from registration. That was the beginning of a rapid decline of health. The next two days I was hospitalized, and came home Friday feeling much better. This positive trend was almost negated by our suspicions of an infection, but it turned out just to be topical. My motto about the cancer experience is quickly becoming, "It's always something." Once you get over the nausea, your counts start to drop, then due to low counts you get sick. Once you are finally starting to feel better from this illness, you have chemo again. If there is a bright side to this, I think I've managed to adopt it: when another problem occurs, don't start acting all surprised, you know things like this are a part of the experience; you knew things like this will happen. It is similar to a teacher telling you they will be giving pop quizzes daily. The quizzes are many, but at least you know they are coming. The period just ended so I have to go. Essay season again and I feel ready.

The beginning of the school year coincided with the beginning of Miles' radiation protocol. This process began with a simulation of the treatment in order to precisely map the tumor location and map the coordinates for the radiation beam. Miles was so thin that he couldn't lay flat on the treatment platform, so they made a custom body mold to give him support. This delayed the scheduled start of the radiation treatment and, because they didn't want him to have to endure both radiation and chemo simultaneously, it also delayed his next chemo round. This gave Miles a chance to recover a normal appetite for food, and he did so with gusto, as reported in his September 20 update:

The best part about the chemo getting postponed was that I was able to eat dinner, and rest assured I made the most out of this opportunity. Guido's pizza. Enough said. I went to pick it up with Nina. The olfactory lure emanating from the box in the back seat was almost enough to cause us to pull over at the nearest side street, engage in a vicious fight to the death, and the victor would eat the pizza. We got home and rushed inside, backpacks and school things cast aside as we rounded on the steaming pizza. It was hot to the point where you aren't sure if it burns more than its worth but you keep eating anyway; the cheese unmanageably yet delightfully stretchy. For awhile we all just ate standing up by the pizza. Primitive instinct told us we must keep close guard over our food in case predators tried to steal it from us. Eventually we mustered up the will power to get silverware-- pointless devices invented by high society to hamper the rate of food consumption--and sit down. Bare hands proved more expedient. In this fashion, we ate to our hearts content.

It may not have been with pizza, but I'd bet most of you have had a dining experience reminiscent of this. Instinct takes over; table manners are thrown to the winds. Not much to learn about life from that pizza story I guess, but I had fun writing it. Catch you all later.

Miles' readers were delighted to hear that he was enjoying a normal teenager's appetite. Jonny Immerman's comment was reflective of the readers' happiness for Miles:

September21, 2005 "LOVE THE GOOD ENERGY. Keep up with the good thoughts and good energy buddy... pizza or whatever it is that's making you smile, just keep focusing on it just like you're doing... i could feel the positivity and strength coming out of you from that writing... felt great to feel it... stay strong buddy and keep that chin up boss. Jonny"

The docs decided to stage the next round of chemo before the beginning of radiation. The chemo brought Miles back to nausea land, so with his permission, Nancy handled his next update. She told of the intense response she witnessed when a nurse spilled a few drops of the chemo drug onto the floor:

September27, 2005

Miles has given me permission to do his update. He is emerging from the last round of inpatient chemo and getting ready for radiation. Now that he is in school, he has to ready himself for classes the second he catches his breath. We had an experience in the hospital that in my view was powerful. Miles had completed the required six hour hydration period prior to receiving cytoxan. This process is necessary because the chemo drugs can burn the bladder. Yes. The nurse then hung the bag of chemo on the IV pole and a few drops of chemo drug accidently spilled on to the floor. She immediately stepped back and threw several towels (which were later discarded) on the few drips. She then called someone from "Environmental Services" who arrived promptly, wearing large rubber gloves, and carrying a mop with strong detergent. What was striking about this picture was that no one flinched when the entire contents of the bag of this toxic substance was dripped into Miles' body. One day, years from now, we will look back at these days of cancer treatment and view them as barbaric. Now that I've been up close and personal, I already do so. Nancy

It was the end of September, 2005, the end of the Jewish year, and the end of Miles' fifth round of VAC. It was difficult to comprehend that we had been members of the cancer club for only four months. So much had transpired since that Saturday in June when Miles and I were expecting to attend the father-son driving school. Our world had been turned about on its axis. The prideful had been humbled, the strong made weak, the fearless frightened.

CHAPTER FOUR

PRAYERS

Just as Miles returned to school to start the eleventh grade, he also started a five-week series of daily radiation treatments, which began immediately after the school day ended. The chemo regimen also continued unabated. The combination of school, radiation, and chemo left Miles demonstrably weakened. I recall feeling such sorrow, pity and foreboding at the sounds of retching emanating from the privacy of his bathroom. He must have felt as awful as it's possible to feel, short of some forms of cruel torture. Eventually, on September 30, 2005, it was necessary to admit him to Beaumont Hospital because of his nausea, vomiting, abdominal pain and weight loss. Blood studies also showed him to have a low neutrophil count.

After consultation with Dr. Gebara, a pediatric gastroenterologist, it was decided to place a feeding tube, or Gastro-tube, through Miles' abdomen and directly into his stomach. This would permit the introduction of nutritional supplements into the digestive system without the consequence of nausea and vomiting. In terms of the way he felt, this time was a new low for Miles. Over the course of the next five weeks, there were only three days when Miles felt "normal." Although he described his feelings to his CarePage readers, he never complained! He understood that these awful feelings were part of the cost of the effort to save his life. His acceptance of the treatments meant acceptance of the side effects as well. Miles knew of cases where kids his age, rather than suffer its side effects, had voluntarily discontinued treatment. Knowing his chances were slim even with treatment, he'd decided to go for it – to shoot for the one-in-five chance, to try to thread the eye of the needle. But by mid-October, Miles' spirits were so low that Nancy made a plea to his readers:

This is the mom typing, MILES' MOM. Now is the time for me to fulfill the maternal impulse of protection. Now is the time for me to ask all of you to send a message to Miles. He may be angry with me for going public with his current state, but that's a chance I'll have to take. Miles is now nearly half way through radiation. The effects are cumulative. He received his chemo treatment last night. It was and is brutal. The chemo drugs on top of a radiated digestive system are an experience that few have had, even those who have received cancer treatment. It is pain that few can tolerate. It is not for the faint of heart. Going to the hospital yesterday, knowing what he had to endure, was one of the low points of this entire experience - for Miles, and for me, as his mother. The next month will continue to present an increasing and enormous challenge -to his body, to his will, and to his spirit. He will be in the hospital for at least five days as he is going to receive nutritional supplementation to help him fight the good fight. All types of encouragement - messages on this site (he will see them) as well as cards would be appreciated. I know that you pray for Miles. Now I ask you to express to him your encouragement and support. We all need it. Thank you.

His readers and others responded with prayers. A woman who volunteered in the Beaumont Hospital Radiology Department, asked Nancy for Miles' name so that she could pray for him. She said to Nancy, "I see a lot of patients here, but I don't see many kids. For some reason your son has really touched me. Last week in church I wanted to pray for him, but I didn't know his name." She then confided, "I just looked up and said, 'God, you know who I'm talking about.'" Online, prayers were offered from Chicago, New York, Washington, D.C., and the Ukraine, Israel, Tokyo, Saudi Arabia and other distant places.

Nancy had concluded that the success rate using VAC in cases as severe as Miles' were not promising. She began searching for physicians using protocols other than VAC. She learned of a Dr. Nachman, at the University of Chicago, who had developed his own aggressive five-drug protocol. His combination of drugs included Doxorubicin, a drug whose side effects could be so pronounced that the drug earned the nickname the Red Devil. New therapies, not widely available during Miles' illness, promise to be more precise and subtle, such as proton beam therapy, laser knives, and drugs delivered using tumor-specific antigens, or other markers allowing for focused rather than generalized drug delivery. But Miles was treated primarily with systemic drugs that had been in use for decades. There just had not been any breakthroughs in the fight against rhabdomyosarcoma, an orphan disease which affects only a few hundred people every year in this country, primarily children.

A visit to Dr. Nachman's offices at the University of Chicago was set for mid-November. From June through October, Miles had a relatively uneventful course of treatment. He was tolerating chemo, staying on schedule and hadn't had any infections. But the burdens of treatment were accumulating, and the five-day-a-week radiation schedule and the subsequent nausea was fatiguing. The radiation field extended from his pelvis to his chest. The treatment upset his digestive system; he couldn't even tolerate Jell-O. Miles described himself as being in a "constant 'blah' state". His appetite had diminished and his weight loss had accelerated to the point that the gastroenterologist, Dr. Gebara, recommended a trial of total parenteral nutrition (TPN). TPN involves administering a nutritional fluid directly into the bloodstream through a mediport in the chest wall. TPN requires extreme precision in dosing and observing sterile practices. The fluids are given during the night while the patient sleeps. It was decided that I would be trained to hook Miles up to the IV line and start the pump at bedtime, and disconnect him and flush the intravenous lines in the morning. I had already been trained to disconnect him from chemo after a visiting nurse had started it at home.

With all of the ports and tube placements, blood draws, endoscopy, radiation, chemo, transfusions, pill swallowing, contrast drinks and interruptions of sleep, you'd think a person would scream, cry, or go crazy. Not only did Miles retain his sweet temperament; not only did he remain determined to keep up with his classmates in school; not only did he comply with everything asked of him by the medical profession, but he did so without a single complaint. I couldn't do that. Few of us could.

Our mid-November drive to the University of Chicago gave us an understanding of how the "gales of November" were able to sink the Edmund Fitzgerald, the iron ore carrier made famous by musician Gordon Lightfoot. Wind-driven snow and sleet pelted us continuously as we drove along Interstate 94. We arrived around 11:00 p.m. at a modest hotel within walking distance of the University of Chicago Hospital. Little did we know that the Chicago visit would be the origin of another storm in Miles' journey.

The following morning, when Miles had his shirt off in an exam room, one of the nurses thought that the bandage over the port was a little tired looking. The external tubing leading into Miles chest through the mediport, and the overlying bandage, required regular periodic renewal in order to prevent infection. We agreed with the nurse that it should be changed. She went to collect the necessary materials but reported that she didn't have the same type of coupling at the external end of the tube that hooked up to the fluids. A Y-shaped, double-chamber coupling was available, but not a single-chamber coupling like the ones we'd been using; she said it wouldn't make a difference, and we didn't object. After examining Miles and reading his history, Dr. Nachman agreed to design one of his aggressive chemo protocols for him, to be administered by Beaumont Hospital in Michigan.

Upon returning to Michigan, we continued to use the Y-shaped coupling to administer Miles' TPN. Little did we know that the two-chamber coupling was not as easy to keep clean as the single-chamber. At Miles' bedtime on the Monday after Thanksgiving, I hooked him up to his TPN and said goodnight. About fifteen minutes later I heard him anxiously calling me. I went to his room and found him sitting up in bed shaking and shivering uncontrollably, as one might do when very cold. He said he couldn't stop and asked what was going on. Miles vomited and complained of back pain. The TPN had already been brought to room temperature, so it wasn't that the liquid was too cold. All I knew is that we had a medical emergency on our hands. When Nancy and Nina came to find out what was going on, I said, "Nancy, call 911 and request an ambulance." Nancy hesitated only a moment and then went off to make the call.

An ambulance arrived within ten minutes. Miles was still shivering, but less so. The ambulance crew decided he wasn't in extremis and took a number of vital sign readings and filled out some forms. I remained outwardly calm but was very eager to see this crew move quickly through their protocol. Eventually they put him on a gurney and took him downstairs to the ambulance. I was invited to join them as they transported him to Beaumont's Emergency Room. After the paperwork, a visit from an intern, and a blood draw, the chief ER physician on duty arrived to assess Miles. She examined him and told us that her working hypothesis was that he was experiencing a form of septic shock and would need to be admitted to receive IV antibiotics. The infection was suspected as being attributable to a contaminated bag of TPN, or a contaminated line into his mediport. The likelihood of a contaminated bag was quite low, the likelihood of a contaminated line much greater. In the half year since Miles' cancer was discovered, this was the scariest incident for me. Retrospectively, I felt I should have questioned the use of a different type of coupling by the nurse in Chicago. One of the doctors on our team in Detroit should have been consulted about that change of device, by either me or the nurse. Also, I should have been re-trained on how to flush a two-chamber device, as opposed to a single-chamber one. Perhaps I had become complacent and less vigilant.

Fortunately the antibiotics were effective and Miles returned home a few days later. Until this incident, I had been under the radar on the CarePage website. Nancy and Miles authored all of the patient updates. I had perhaps written one update in the entire first six months. Most of my contributions to the CarePage were posted among messages made by readers. But Nancy's brother, Wayne, who had been in Detroit for Thanksgiving with his wife, Nancy, and their daughters, Sophie and Tess, decided to shine a light on me by posting a comment that praised my handling of this particular medical crisis.

I responded with appreciation for Wayne's flattering comments but said it was Miles who immediately came to mind when I came across this quote from Euripides:

"This is courage...to bear unflinchingly what heaven sends."

Miles found, earned, and owns a level of courage beyond any that has been demanded of me in my half century.

Aside from saying some nice things about me, Wayne's comments highlighted two other facets of our journey. Firstly, Wayne's ability to express himself, in words or music, reaches a very high level. His contributions over the course of our journey helped us to understand and crystallize the deep human dimensions of our ugly blessing. Wayne's involvement in our drama, as brother to Nancy and uncle to Miles, also reached a very high level of commitment. He was deeply admired by Miles and they formed a special bond, different in many ways from even a good father-son relationship. It was a relationship only a talented, dedicated uncle and mature nephew can know. One made all the more translucent when seen against the dark clouds on the horizon. Secondly, Wayne underscored in his tribute to me the fact that, to be most effective, families must act as a team in challenging cancer; each team member contributing from his or her core strengths and abilities. He demonstrated that there is a role on such a team for extended family – for uncles, cousins, grandparents, and others. From pills to pillows to prayers, there is a role for everyone.

CHAPTER FIVE

A TEACHER TO ALL

By November of 2005, with six months of experience under our belt, we'd accumulated enough experience with Miles' affliction and its treatment to give us the sense that we could handle our new reality. We'd learned to anticipate, or accept, sudden curves and steep descents. We were a little less fearful. Miles called his cancer a journey, and I think at this point he believed that the journey would end favorably for him. On November 28, he'd had the surgery to insert a "G-tube". This gastric tube went directly into his stomach so that he could be fed nutrients without the risks we had experienced with TPN. And the potential side-effect of nausea was also eliminated. Miles was grateful and hopeful. He wrote:

> The other day I was just sitting in my room alone, looking out the window and starting to feel sorry for myself. I still had the 103 degree fever and felt pretty miserable. But what I remembered is that there couldn't be a better candidate to have cancer than me. My body is young; we have insurance to enable me to get lifesaving treatment, which some people do not have; we have money beyond what insurance covers, to seek out the opinions of experts like Dr. Nachman, which not everyone can afford to do; I have a mom who has dedicated herself to finding out everything she can and a dad capable of making hard decisions in times of crisis; and I have a helpful sister, supportive friends and an accommodating school.

The truth was that this young man was becoming increasingly dependent upon, and subject to, medical intervention. There is a Jewish prayer, said first thing in the morning, which thanks God for the fact that all of our orifices that should be closed are closed and all that should be open are open, that everything is functioning as it should. In Miles' case this was becoming a wish rather than a thanksgiving. But buoying him up in light of the facts was an important team effort, and cancer survivor Jonny Immerman was part of that team:

November 29, 2005 "Hey buddy, that last paragraph you wrote just brought tears to my eyes. You've got it right. Exactly right. You get it. And that understanding is a key reason why you're going to get through this and live a wonderful life ahead. You're there mentally. You're all the way there. Now just get through each day one at a time buddy….you're doing great!"

After the G-tube surgery, Miles stayed in the hospital to begin the five-drug Nachman chemotherapy protocol. This inpatient stay lasted twelve days and was such an intense round of chemo that, by December 5, Miles remarked that:

> This whole cancer thing has become much more of a full-time commitment over the past month. I used to have some good days and some bad days then still other mediocre days. The three week interval between each chemo round always contained a light at the end of tunnel, promising that within those three weeks, at some point or another, I would feel remnants of health once more. Hopefully I am wrong, but this no longer seems to be the case. I've been unwell pretty much continuously throughout this past month: the esophagitis, not being able to walk from the infected hip, the blood infection, surgery and then right into this last chemo.

Despite his continuously feeling unwell, he had no malice against the cancer itself. On December 20 he wrote:

> Some people depict cancer cells as destroying with a sense of malice. I disagree…. I am more forgiving of the cancer cells than Lance Armstrong, reasoning that they cannot be held accountable for their actions since they are merely cellular processes, copying their DNA as any other cell would, except that the copy they are given is corrupted. The corruption of the DNA was not done deliberately by my body to spite me for eating McDonalds or not wearing a jacket, it just happened. The cells have no conscience either, so how they can be considered as acting with malice (even though their actions are destructive) any more than the molecules of water in an ocean can be considered malicious when they drown someone?

Was it accurate to say that Miles' cancer "had just happened"? Was Miles' affliction due purely to chance, to genetics, to environment, to divine intervention? We don't know. As for genetics, I've heard it said about cancer that "genetics loads the gun and the environment pulls the trigger." Miles attributed his suffering to random chance, accepted it as his life's course, and resolved to make the most of it in whatever time he had left.

His readers sensed the deepening of his insight and responded, in their own styles, with their own deeper thoughts:

KarenMelaas, December 3, 2005 "I strongly sense that you have had the effect of bringing many of us to open our eyes, our hearts and our minds far more fully. While you may have feelings of weakness, you are indeed a pillar of strength.

Please count me among those who continue to share hopes with others, prayers with G-d, each and every day that your health will steadily and sturdily improve, Miles. You bring extraordinary light to all of us. Thank you for sharing yourself and your experiences so articulately and with such beautiful voice."

Peggy Daitch, December 05, 2005 "Miles, It pains us to read what you have been through. We can only imagine what it does to you!! Your experience and your journal is a gift that gives us perspective on the irritating issues within our own lives (Cancun wedding cancelled due to hurricane Wilma is a good example!). Your courage, optimism and poetic philosophy are instructive to all of us. While our hearts reach out to you and try to lift you up, you are instead lifting us up! We only hope we can offer you a fraction of the buoyancy you have given back..Thank you! Love, Peggy."

As for fractions, it might be said that Miles was only living a normal life every third week. The first week was all about treatment, the second week was all about recovery, and the third week was a little taste of normalcy before the next round of chemo began. During that third week Miles squeezed the lemon hard, diving into life, which for him centered on school. This was so apparent that on December 24, at the inception of the Christmas break, the Dean of Students, Charles Shaw, gave Miles his own report card:

Report card for Miles, December 24, 2005 "Although I am not technically one of Miles' classroom teachers, I am in a manner of speaking a teacher of all the students in Cranbrook Kingswood, in my role as head of the upper school. In my last official act in that role in 2005, I hereby submit Miles's report card to the world. I saw Miles make his way back to school one morning in early December with the aid of a cane. He was not aware that we had a different schedule for the day, so he was a whole one hour too early for his class. It suddenly struck me that Miles had one whole unplanned hour in his life before him. I studied his face at that moment. It was a beautiful thing to behold. Miles was very pleased with his discovery of time. We had an excellent chat about his leg and everything else. Miles made me feel wonderful, and I went along with a very capital feeling in my heart all day. He had declared that he would be fine with this leg thing in a matter of days. The next week he came back to school and in fact his leg was better and he was walking around in holiday radiance. Your report card, Miles: On that day I inducted you, in my heart, into the faculty of Cranbrook Kingswood. You added to my knowledge of hope and good will. You have spread wisdom all around you and become a teacher to us all. Thank you for taking us all with you. Sincerely, Charles T. Shaw."

CHAPTER SIX

SIGNS OF HOPE

In January of 2006, a major physical assessment, that included full-body CAT and PET scans, brought uplifting news. There was confirmation that the cancer had not spread; vital organs were cancer-free, the areas of tumor had shrunk, and the lymph nodes were no longer enlarged. Nancy posted the following hallelujah:

> We are rejoicing. We are winning the war…bigger than the one with Al-Qaida. That's what our dear GI doc calls it, and that's what it is. And that's the six o'clock news.

But "had not spread" also meant that there were still cancer cells lurking within, despite the treatment which went beyond the standard VAC protocol. All cheerleading aside, the grim prospects did not escape Miles' consciousness. At an age when one might expect the biggest challenge of the day to be a homework assignment, Miles had given himself another assignment. His daily work was to confront reality while pitting his will against that of malicious cells that wanted to take his life. Miles could no longer view mortality as a fuzzy concept to be acknowledged in a dim and distant future. On February 22, 2006, at seventeen-and-a-half years of age, he wrote the following:

> You will be forgotten. It will only take a handful of generations before no one within your own family remembers your name. You will leave behind no legacy except the creation of those who will forget you. But don't feel neglected. You have forgotten your ancestors as well. You have eight great-grandparents, how many of them can you name? When is the last time you visited a grandparent's gravestone? Now my intentions here are not to guilt-trip you into going to the cemetery. I am passing no judgment because, quite simply, life goes on for everybody. There will always

be winter and it will always be followed by spring. Life and death, life and death. The ones forgetting will be the ones forgotten.

Yet isn't it somehow a twisted comfort to know that however big a mess you make with your life, the Great Cosmic Order will remain intact? On the other hand, this means that you are totally insignificant and your existence could be near meaningless. If, in a century from now, you are virtually forgotten by your own family, what does this say about your impact on broader echelons of your community? What are you (even in life) to your city, your country, your planet, your galaxy? You will soon be forgotten. Does this scare you or comfort you?

What did Miles have to look forward to after writing the previous post? He had a date with Doxorubicin, the Red Devil, of which he wrote on the eighth of March:

This is the last of the really nasty chemo rounds. I would have thought it would be easier to go into this one knowing it's the last, but it's been just as hard. It's a sense of dread. That's the best adjective to describe the morning of a chemo round. Everyone struggles from a lack of inertia in the morning, but it gets amplified many times on days like these. Standing in the shower under a jet of hot water, I give legitimate consideration to just staying there forever, even though I realize the impossibility. It takes superhuman inner strength to reach for that temperature knob, turn off the water and face the day. I'd think many people experience this even on normal days. Now I'm musing off on a tangent. What was I saying?

Yeah, difficulty getting myself to the hospital. In the parking lot I feel this wild compulsion to just run away from the hospital. Just start running. There are these woods nearby, I'd go there first, and then...I don't know, try and hitch a ride far away to some small town in Iowa, keep a low profile and live off the land.

Right now I am only steps away from the pediatric doors. Once I cross over I cannot come back out without a doctor's orders. This update ends here. This is my last chance to make a break for Iowa.

It was every bit as bad as anticipated. While he was still undergoing the infusion, Nancy wrote:

March 9, 2006 CALLING ALL SUPPORTERS - MILES NEEDS YOUR MESSAGES: Miles had good reason to dread this round. I'm not exaggerating when I say that Miles has been in hell for two days, with one more day to go. This was the first time in this journey that I heard him utter (in sheer agony) that he can't go on much longer. He did have one moment of lucidity this afternoon, and expressed an interest in his messages on his CarePage. The moment was short-lived, however, so he never retrieved them. Miles needs you now! This is not the time for reticence. Even a word or two would be fantastic. Let's inundate him with encouragement and validation. I know he'll appreciate it.

Miles was flooded with supporting messages from every quarter – relatives, classmates, friends, friends of friends, rabbis, childhood chums, and many other readers of his blog. His Uncle Wayne's allegorical contribution was representative of the spirit of the messages:

"Just a few days ago we were sitting together in the second row mid-court watching the Michigan vs. Indiana basketball game. These were the best seats I've ever had to anything. We were pulling for Michigan all the way. But we could see that Indiana had the strongest player. We didn't know his name. He wore Number 5. Michigan jumped out to a big lead, and led the entire game. Indiana was always down, but never out. Number 5 was patient. He kept plugging away. In the final minute, with the last game of the season on the line and his team behind, he somehow fought back. He dug in, summoned hidden strength, overcame adversity, and vanquished his foe. Indiana won after all. Everyone in the stadium was shocked. But we knew better.

I'm thinking about you now, Miles, and Number 5. I see you slamming that big basket and stealing this game, too. Even when you're down, we know better."

Miles finished the chemo round on March tenth, and then laid low for the next five days. On March fifteenth he felt rested and posted an update to thank his readers, telling them that they had come through for him in a big way. The next day we took him to the hospital and found that he had severely low hemoglobin and neutrophil counts. This resulted in a four-day inpatient admission for blood transfusions and observation. It was more of the cancer pattern we knew well: treatment/recovery/living – treatment/recovery/living.

Nancy continued her research to learn more about cancer. She identified cancer-oriented "centers of excellence", relevant drug trials, national review boards, cancer websites, and specialized chat rooms. It was in a chat room devoted to Rhabdo that Nancy learned about Dr. Leonard Wexler, a pediatric oncologist at Memorial Sloan Kettering Cancer Center (MSKCC). Dr. Wexler had made a specialty of treating children and adolescents with bone and soft tissue cancer. He had built a team of oncologists, surgeons, and radiation therapists who specialized in newly-diagnosed and recurrent sarcomas. A graduate of the Boston University School of Medicine, with a residency at the Albert Einstein College of Medicine, and a National Cancer Institute Fellowship, Dr. Wexler had earned a reputation as a physician with a rare combination of high intelligence, dedication, and excellent patient rapport.

Nancy placed a call to Dr. Wexler's office and set up a telephone interview with him. During the subsequent interview, she provided Dr. Wexler with a comprehensive history of Miles' case. As a result of the phone interview, Dr. Wexler invited Nancy and Miles to come to MSKCC in New York City for an evaluation. He asked for documents and scans to be sent ahead. An appointment was set for March 26, 2006. Miles' blood counts were so low that he was given a transfusion of platelets the day before the flight so that he could tolerate the lower oxygen level in the aircraft's cabin.

Nancy and Miles had a very productive first meeting with Dr. Wexler. They were very impressed with his attentiveness, rapport, and keen mind. To assess the impact of prior treatment, as well as measure Miles' current tumor burden, Dr. Wexler ordered a scan using a radioactive contrast dye that Miles had to drink before laying down in a very confined space. Miles later described this imaging test as a procedure which "took not-fun to a whole new level". But Dr. Wexler's evaluation of the results was useful in that they indicated a need for additional radiation treatment of some cancerous nodes found above a line of demarcation.

While the discovery of additional cancerous areas was a setback, we could only move forward. We were happy to have added Dr. Wexler to the team. In fact, he was essentially appointed captain, as Miles wrote on March 30, 2006:

You want to know how the consult with Dr. Wexler went. Thankfully it went well; because he is going to be the ultimate authority in call the shots now. What he says goes. In Wexler We Trust. I would trust him with my life, which in this case is not just a saying---it's literal. My mom and I agree, he is excellent in all aspects a patient looks for in a doctor.

As things stood before our consult, I had two more months of chemo. The question was what comes next: Nothing? Something? If we were to do more treatment, we were considering surgery, bone marrow transplant, more chemo, or a combination. Surgery and BMT are not going to happen, at least not at this point in the game. However, I will be tacking on another four months of more chemo. I'll be taking a drug I haven't used before, Irinotecan. For the first round (three weeks) I will probably stay at the Ronald McDonald house here in New York. I'm not disappointed in this latest development and this has nothing to do with my attitude. It has to do with the survival statistics, which are not very encouraging, and my hope of getting any edge I can. Also, the radiologists here at Sloan discovered that I may have had some cancerous lymph nodes that were not irradiated. If this is the case, I will probably be receiving another five or six weeks of radiation.

With all of that in Miles lap, the likelihood of previous medical oversights, the prospect of extended treatments, Miles was still able to enjoy a bite of the Big Apple, going to the play "Doubt", eating at different ethnic restaurants with cousins, taking the subway, and so on. When Miles returned to Michigan, he digested all he had learned to date, and decided to up the ante with his CarePage readers:

April 8, 2006, Whew, this one's gonna be big. This is probably the most important update and the biggest step in my relationship with my readers to date. Brace yourself for this one.

I've decided to share something with you. I've decided to share it in light of my great uncle, Bryce Alpern's, funeral this upcoming Sunday. I've been contemplating whether or not to make it public for some time now. I'm talking about the statistics, the hard numbers. I don't know why the passing of my uncle has compelled me to finally share it, I think seeing all my relatives flying in for a funeral has brought a harsh immediacy to my own situation. I've decided to be completely upfront and brutally honest with you all because I feel that as people in my life, you deserve to know.

Rhabdomyosarcoma is unlike lymphoma or breast cancer, leukemia or testicular cancer in that it is not something which most people survive. It's only found in young people and it's a cancer for which relatively little progress has been made. I guess there's no easy way to say it so I'll just say it: the overall five year survival rate for Stage IV Alveolar Rhabdomyosarcoma is about 20%. So there it is. I suppose I have a slight leg-up on that number because I have achieved a CR, or complete response to the treatment---which not everyone does. But this advantage should not be overstated as only a small minority actually die in treatment or do not achieve a CR.

Most people are like me. Rhabdo is extremely responsive to chemotherapy, so most kids go through the course, achieve clear scans, and then wait and pray. The problem is that very frequently there are sub-detectable levels of cancer remaining, the toughest .1% that withstood the chemotherapy and radiation. These super-cells (possibly cancer stem cells) begin to regrow, leading to relapse in the other 78% or so of the kids. The combination of these Darwinian selected super-cells and the decreased ability of the body to withstand another round of such intensive treatment are nearly always fatal. This means that even if I can say my scans show no cancer, I am by no means in the clear. The waiting phase that will follow the treatment phase is the real test. So...yeah, it's a lot to take in. It's hard to even conceive, let alone accept. I don't know what ballpark you thought my odds were in previously, I would think higher than this but maybe not. Please excuse my lack of tact, I'm really ripping off the band-aid here and now the wound is exposed.

Although the situation seems pretty dismal, there is good news. I HAVE responded very well to treatment, and I'm receiving world-class care here at Beaumont and under Dr. Wexler's guidance at Sloan Kettering. If I had to have cancer, I could not have picked a better time in history or place in the world to have it. It's not hopeless, but 5:1 against is pretty scary. There's no pressure on you to comment, I don't know what I would tell me either. I know some of you might say that my chances aren't 20%, they are 100-or-nothing. That is true, but statistics are not completely arbitrary and I just thought you deserved to know what I'm up against.

For all the downsides of having cancer, it does have the positive of effect of bringing people in my life closer to me and me closer to them, and that's something I've really valued. Friendship is forged from the hard stuff.

With his life in the balance, Miles had acquired a deep appreciation for relationships and an appetite for connection, which he was able to savor the following week at the family's Passover Seder:

I was able to make it to our annual Seder. It's a big thing with lots of family flying in from all over the country. On second thought, I guess everybody's Seder is annual. After the Seder, I slept over at the hotel where all my cousins were staying. It was something that, even while it's happening, you know it will be something that stays imprinted in your memory for years to come--- a remember-the-time-in-the-making. Lots of stuff happening this week too. As a matter of fact, I can't say there has been a dull moment once this year. There have been some hard moments as well as some good ones, but not a dull one. So while in many respects this has been the worst year of my life, I don't think I can say I've ever been more alive. Sublime ups, staggering downs. And that's living, man. Depression is no fun, but at least you feel *something*.

The pace of time was picking up for Miles and he noticed it. He was scheduled to make a second visit to Dr. Wexler on April 27, 2006. On the evening prior to his departure he wrote:

April 26, 2006

It never ceases to amaze me how quickly the future becomes the past. Even times that move at a crawling pace while they are happening are behind you before you know it. The school year always flies by. My teenage years are flying by. I've wondered if elderly people feel like childhood was yesterday. How did I get here so fast? How can I hold on to the time I have in front of me, especially if there's not much left? It's like trying to cup water in your hands. It's gonna slide no matter what you do so just do your best to make it count and enjoy it while it lasts.

I can remember June, 2005. I can remember thinking that 42 weeks of chemo was an eternity. It was forever. I'll be reaching forever in about two and a half weeks. I can remember being unconfident. I remember feeling like I was being asked to do something I was not strong enough to do. I still think I'm being asked to deal with a hell of a lot at seventeen, but there's a certain confidence instilled by persevering through 40 weeks of chemotherapy and 30 treatments of radiation. The fact is, we rise to the occasion. There was a child whose leg was crushed under the wheel of a car, so the mother singlehandedly took hold of the back bumper and lifted the end of the car into the air. That is superhuman. Our potential is dizzying.

On a more immediate note, I leave for New York tomorrow - 8+ days. We're going back to see Wexler for some more diagnostics and potentially surgery. (Hopefully not.) The surgery/no surgery decision is undoubtedly the most important one of my life to date. I'm not sure how to properly convey how overwhelming that is. And this next part is going to sound trivial after all that, but I have some very exciting Yankees game plans. I can't wait. I'll be sure do an update.

It's time to finish packing. I'll update from New York. Be well.

Miles' one-week trip to New York City was full of rewards from beginning to end. He and Nancy checked into the Ronald McDonald House on the Upper East Side. The activities of the following day were arranged by Sandy and Scott, close friends of Wayne's spouse, Miles' Aunt Nancy. As Miles described it:

Sandy and Scott arranged a whole day for us. And what a day it was! We were taken by limo to a Yankees game against the Toronto Blue Jays. After the game (and after a hot dog, slice of pizza, cotton candy, etc.) we got back in the limo and went home. But it didn't end there my friends. After quickly changing, we got back in the limo and went to dinner at Tavern on the Green. Several of us, including myself, got the seafood sampler appetizer. After that I had steak. After that I had desert. After that I didn't eat for a couple days. To Scott and Sandy, your thank you note is on the way. I can't do a proper thank you right here because it would span more characters than I'm allowed. Let me just say you've truly created what will be a long-lasting and fond memory. Royalty doesn't live this well.

What did Miles know of royalty? Well, he knew a little about Hamlet, Prince of Denmark. Miles' teachers had begun to display sensitivity to Miles situation, not only in their working around his spotty attendance, but in the nature of the assignments they gave him. In April, 2006, he was enrolled in a class entitled "Literary Traditions". His teacher, Ms. Rubinstein, gave him the challenging assignment of reading Shakespeare's "Hamlet". I cannot help but think that she was fully aware of the profound effect that Miles' reading of Hamlet's deep meditations on death would have on him. In the paper Miles turned in, it is apparent that the segments on death were well read. Miles describes Hamlet's "dramatic transformation regarding his attitude towards life and death", accepting "death as inevitable and … beyond his ability to control". Miles quoted the famous passages:

"To die, to sleep - No more - and by a sleep to say we end the heartache…that flesh is heir to."

"If it be not now, yet it will come…Since no man of aught he leaves knows what is't to betimes. Let be."

"The readiness is all."

Miles concludes his paper by writing, "By the end of the play, Hamlet no longer fears death nor yearns for it like before. He is finally comfortable in a position of powerlessness, of not knowing when or how death will come for him or what it will hold in store."

Whatever it held in store did not seem ready for immediate delivery as the results of the New York visit brought uplifting news to all of us. An encouraged Miles wrote on May 7, 2006:

May 7, 2006

The biopsy came back completely clean; there will be no surgery in the forseeable future!

(!!#%*)@$%&$*&$^$%^#$!@T%Y^!)

I am returning home from New York under the very best possible circumstances. Detecting cancer can be done through one of two methods: imaging (such as x-ray, CT, MRI, PET, etc.) or biopsy (taking a tissue sample and looking at it under a microscope). My imaging results showed one remaining ambiguous area at the original site. This could have been either dead cancer cells, scar tissue from radiation, active cancer, or any combination. The biopsy in New York was the last and, in many ways, most definitive piece of the puzzle. And it came back clean. So what does all of this mean? A couple people have asked if this means I can stop treatment now. From a quality of life perspective, it means everything. It means no surgery, no removing organs, no scars. I can't understate how relieved I am about that. On another level, it means that, to the best of technological ability, no cancer can be found in my body. Now I hate to be a downer but here is where I have to be. There is a caveat. The "to the best of technological ability" part is operative. I've said before that most kids make it to this point, seemingly cancer-free, but there are still sub-detectable levels of cancer tumor remain, or what are called micro-mets---small clusters of distant, metastatic cancer cells (i.e. a rhabdo cell or two insidiously hiding out in, say, the lungs). So while I'm heading in the right direction, I'm by no means out of the woods. But then again, I can't ask for anything more than to be heading in the right direction. What comes next in terms of treatment? Tomorrow morning I go into the hospital for a five-day stay, the last round of my original treatment plan. But as I've informed you already, there is more to come. The radiology guys at Sloan found out that the guys at Beaumont missed some areas in their radiation plan and left some malignant lymph nodes unirradiated….. Luckily, luckily, so very luckily, it was caught. A stitch in time saves…everything. I will be receiving more radiation to my upper chest/throat area. My hospital friend, Ryan, had radiation to his throat and couldn't eat or swallow for weeks, and didn't regain taste for months after that. So it doesn't look like much of a picnic.

After the six weeks of radiation (projected to end late June), I'll be going back to New York to pilot the new Irinotecan chemotherapy, which I will be doing probably through October. That's the extent of the foreseeable future.

A foreseeable future, that's what we wanted for Miles, for him to be looking ahead. Here he was, closing in on the first year of treatment, weeks away from the completion of his 11th grade at Cranbrook, days away from the completion of his status as a Beaumont pediatric patient. He had things to say about all of this. About the Beaumont pediatric ward he said:

> Crazy as it sounds, I'm going to miss this place. I've spent a good part of the last 10 months here, and if you spend that much time anywhere, it grows on you. I'm friendly with all the nurses. I know which of the two pantries is more likely to be stocked with chocolate milk. The dietician doesn't even have to ask if I'd like Spaghetti-o's anymore, she just brings them. I know from which rooms I can tap into the wireless internet from the adult floor overhead, and which rooms I cannot. I've made friends here who can understand what I'm dealing with on a level that none of my healthy friends or healthy adults could.

June 4, 2006 was the first anniversary of our entry into the cancer club. It was on that date in 2005 that Miles had had the abdominal pain which led to an Emergency Room admission and, eventually, to his cancer diagnosis. In an ironic alignment of the stars, it was also National Cancer Survivors Recognition Day. At this juncture, Miles had no evidence of disease and was about to switch from a multi-drug chemotherapy to a single-drug maintenance regimen, on Irinotecan. As we approached summer, both the treatment burden and the academic burden were lightening. Miles was coming up for air and sunshine. In assessing the prior year's impact on him, he composed one of the more memorable CarePage updates from which the following is extracted:

> I have had a chance---for really the first time in my life---to be inspirational. It's not something most teenagers can lay claim to. Not because they are incapable of inspirational feats, but simply because, for those first parts of life, most young people do not come across an opportunity to really show what they're made of and inspire and teach others. Getting this chance, and from what I've been told, succeeding, has been a true privilege and an honor. (I guess when things aren't going so well in your own life, go altruistic.)
>
> There is a feeling that even if I die, I've already made my time here count for something. That in some way or another, I've meant something to a lot of people, and changed them---if only a little.....getting a chance to live in my life, as well as indirectly in (hopefully) all 268 of these CarePage readers and countless others,

knowingly and unknowingly, across the world, has made it all worthwhile.

Nobody knows for sure what we're doing here, or how to gauge our successfulness, but I tend to think that if you leave the world a better place than when you got here, as much as was personally possible, you're doing pretty good.

Taking that as the quantification of success, you then realize that your biological vitality means very little---having a beating heart and operational lungs does not define you, your effect on the world around you does. Once you fulfill that service, your shift is done; you're off work and it's time to go home. So you don't necessarily need a lot of years to have a lot of effect. In fact, maybe the opposite: if the good die young, it is they who have the most profound effect of all. If you can truly embrace this---and I'm still trying---that's sainthood.

It takes the darkest, bleakest of human tribulations to bring out the best in us. It is in the face of hopelessness more than any other time that we unite and rally around what is really important. If I have to be a martyr for that to happen, then I will do my best to try and accept that. The only thing that's real is the intangible.

A year into his illness, Miles had acquired 268 CarePage readers, a number sufficient to give him the sense that he was having an impact. We had no idea that greater success was on the horizon.

CHAPTER SEVEN

SUMMER OF LOVE

One day I noticed sudden changes Miles had made in his bedroom décor. These changes were evidence of a new cultural perspective on his part. He was growing in knowledge about both his world and the larger world. What had I noticed? In the corner of his room, above his bed, were mounted two movie posters. One was a poster from a James Bond movie, showing actress Halle Berry and Pierce Brosnan in defiant poses. The other poster showed actress Angelina Jolie in a skintight suit as character Lara Croft in the movie "Tomb Raider".

Then one day, in the spring of 2006, I was surprised to find that the posters had been changed. The James Bond and Lara Croft posters had been taken down and two new ones put up. One of the new posters showed a young Bob Dylan standing in a recording studio, guitar in hand, staring pensively at the fingerboard of his guitar. The other poster showed a caricature of Hunter Thompson, author of Fear and Loathing in Las Vegas, wearing mirrored aviator glasses which reflected the Las Vegas strip. Miles had read the book as a school assignment, and had seen the movie several times. To me this indicated that he had graduated from admiring fictitious superheroes to admiring real people who had achieved greatness in their fields. It also implied that Miles had aspirations. He was looking beyond the disease. One element which explained his new outlook was his experimentation with some legal mind-altering drugs, salvia and morning glory. He had asked me for permission and I gave it to him, for many reasons. Under normal circumstances, the parents of a seventeen-year-old would typically be concerned, watchful, strict, and restrictive about such things. In our case, fearing that Miles might not be allotted a full portion of life, we wanted him, with discretion, to experience whatever he wanted to experience. This is also why we were so receptive and accommodating when Miles asked us to steer clear of the first floor of the house when he had girlfriends to the house.

Now receiving only a single drug, Irinotecan, Miles was looking and feeling good. His hair was growing back and he sported a goatee. His classmate and friend, Monica, had been invited to the house to make peanut butter fudge one afternoon. When she came over, Nancy and I were briefly introduced. After greeting Monica, we excused ourselves as she and Miles took over the kitchen. We did our best to stay out of sight, but sounds reached us in other rooms. And it was such a joy to hear the two teens laughing and making small talk while reading the recipe, assembling and measuring the ingredients. Fudge making requires care in bringing sugar to precise temperatures. Having worked with Bunsen burners and chemicals in their school lab, they were quite adept and made a good batch of fudge. It was just so precious to have Miles engaged in a prosaic chore, at home, with a girlfriend.

Miles was well-liked by all who met him, not only because of his reputation for battling cancer, but also because he was good-looking, athletic, had a scintillating verbal humor, and was full of gentle compassion. He was known for his comforting hugs and his honesty, reliability, good judgment, and ability to keep a confidence. He wasn't petty, didn't gossip, always gave the benefit of the doubt, and saw the best in people. Hence, we were not surprised to find girls visiting the house. The week after Monica, it was Julia. Miles and Julia made sushi together. Throughout that summer between his junior and senior years, we caught fleeting glimpses of other friends, of both genders, as they kicked back in the family room or arrived to pick up Miles for a little jaunt. We heard many names, only some of which could we attach to faces – Pavloff, Medwid, Travis, Henrik, Jessie, Kat, Katie, Becky, Sarah, Robyn, and others. The name Robyn was attached to a lovely lady who would eventually rise to a prominent role in Miles' life. Hers was the name from which the space between girl and friend would be dropped. But not before the summer was interrupted by a three-week medical evaluation and treatment episode.

Traveling to New York, Miles spent the first three weeks of July being evaluated by Dr. Wexler and his group at Memorial Sloan Kettering Cancer Center. In addition to looking for tumor activity with magnetic resonance imaging (MRI) and positron emission tomography (PET), the doctors evaluated his vital organ functions and performed a general checkup. While there, Miles also received some chemotherapy in the form of Irinotecan, which is normally well-tolerated, but produced significant nausea and vomiting in Miles. An anti-nausea drug, Palonosetron, was administered to good effect. Ironically, the Palonosetron given for side effects cost more than twice as much as the chemotherapeutic agent itself. Altogether, the outpatient facility and physician charges for that visit amounted to approximately $40,000. The conclusion was that there was no evidence of disease, and that a maintenance regimen would be followed for the time being. With some considerable relief, Miles returned to Detroit to resume the relatively easy life of a student on summer break – which meant pursuing Robyn.

Robyn and her family were recent arrivals to the community, having relocated from New Jersey in 2005. Robyn's father, Patrick, had taken a chief executive job with a local hospital system. Her mother, Laurie, was a homemaker. Pat and Laurie had three daughters, Robyn, Devon, and Rachel. All the girls had distinctive, thick and curly, carrot-colored hair. The family had purchased a large, old wood-frame house on a hill less than a mile from the Cranbrook campus. As a result of Robyn's winning looks and personality, the relaxed and open ambience at her home and its proximity to campus, it had become an after-school hangout for Robyn's friends, which included Miles. After months of being on the receiving end of the generosity and hospitality of Robyn's family, her friends decided to reciprocate by fixing her parents a fancy meal in their house. The evening included candles, music, printed menus, student servers, and multiple courses. On July 29, 2006, Miles described this event in a CarePage update. He wrote, "I sat next to Mrs. W at dinner. She was choked up throughout the entire meal……..were I a parent in her situation, I can only imagine my thought would be, 'with friends like these, my child has turned out alright'---and that's a parent's ultimate goal." At some time during that summer, and I wouldn't have been notified when it happened, Robyn and Miles became a couple, a "thing", as they say. And we would come to know her exceedingly special qualities, and those of her family.

Miles had a round of chemo in early August and then, at Dr. Wexler's sudden urging, Miles decided to attend a week of summer camp in upstate New York. He went to Camp Simcha (joy), operated by an organization named "Chai Lifeline". Nancy described this quickly-arranged episode in an August 10, 2006 CarePage update:

Today is a day to celebrate. Life in the Levin household approached as close to normal as we have known in 15 months. Miles went to camp. Yes, a camp for (Jewish) kids with cancer, but camp. This was put together at record speed. It was arranged, ticket purchased, and out the door in three and a half hours. This is the first time in 15 months that Miles took a plane to somewhere other than a hospital.

Today is a day to celebrate. Miles will mingle with cancer survivors and begin to see himself as one. Others, beyond the CarePage community, will experience the courage, the downright guts that Miles has cultivated and exudes. Others, and many who need it, will feel inspired by his willingness to keep putting one foot in front of the other, one vomit at a time, without a guarantee that it will be worth it. Today is a day for Miles to celebrate his progress and himself.

Today is a day to celebrate. Miles left the nest. The last I heard, he's been sitting for two hours on the runway in New York, waiting for a gate. He's alone, and he can and will manage. My confidence in the separation stems from three factors: 1) he's matured so much in the last year that I have complete confidence in his judgment, 2) he's six days out from chemo, enough time for the poison to lose its grip, at least for the most part, and 3) Dr. Wexler will be there to oversee his care. This is a day to celebrate Miles' return to life, and he's bigger and better.

Today is a day to celebrate all of you companions, true friends, who have walked alongside as we've groped, wailed, stumbled, but, because there is no choice, we've all pressed on.

Today is a day to celebrate life; sometimes, against all odds, life prevails.

Although he felt a little stupid being a camper at age seventeen, Miles found himself enjoying the "boundless contagious energy which quivered electric in the air" at the camp. He made friends, made a sushi platter in the glass fusion workshop, took a helicopter ride, and had a worry-free getaway from his troubles. He was having such a good time that Dr. Wexler suggested he stay a second week. But Miles decided otherwise, as described in a CarePage update on August 24, the night before he would become eighteen-years-old:

... Nearing the end of my week there I was offered the option by Dr. Wexler (who was at the camp) to do a round of treatment and stay (the session was two and a half weeks) but I declined. When you're sick you want to be home.

And so it was. I came home...only to find that my white counts weren't high enough for more chemo. This type of treatment doesn't usually cause significant myelosuppresion (suppression of the bone marrow, the stuff in your bones that makes your blood cells), but oh well.

Anyway, long story short, I was unable to get chemo for an additional and unexpected week and a half. This was enough time off to allow me to regain some of my strength. I mowed the lawn (sounds measly but ask anybody who's been on chemo and it's not). Later in the week, I even took an 18 mile bike ride. 18 miles because---no, I can't believe it either---I turn 18 tomorrow. Unthinkable, but there you have it.

Not only is this milestone meaningful in the standard issue, our-little-Miles-is-growing-up-so-fast way, but I could be dead by now... easily. To be here typing these words to you now is nothing short of a miracle. On top of that, I have no evidence of disease. For once, I'm not quite sure what to say. Whatever happens, I made it to adulthood. There's something good happening here. Anybody think they can guess what my wish was as I blew out the candles?

CHAPTER EIGHT

BACK TO SCHOOL

After Labor Day, Miles began his senior year of high school, taking English, Astronomy, Psychology, Sculpture, and Math. For two weeks out of every three, he would also be undergoing chemotherapy with Irinotecan. It was expected he would be completely finished with cancer treatments by the end of November. Over the previous summer, perhaps through CarePages and word of mouth, the Cranbrook student community had come to a greater appreciation of the severity of Miles' struggle with cancer. In mid-September, he learned that he was one of five finalists nominated by the senior class to be the homecoming king. It didn't hurt his stature, either, that the beautiful Robyn was his queen.

In late September, as Jews celebrated the Jewish New Year and Arabs celebrated Ramadan, Miles wrote a CarePage update that made me very proud in two respects. Firstly, it revealed that he was continuing to grow in consciousness about world affairs and, secondly, because his elegance in English composition was increasingly apparent:

September 23, 2006 at 12:50 AM EDT

To my Jewish readers, "L'shana tova", happy New Year; to my Muslim readers, happy Ramadam.

This morning I was at the hospital and my doctor, a Christian, was telling me about two doctors he used to eat lunch with, an Arab and a Jew, who discovered in conversations that their religions had more similarities than differences. This afternoon I was talking with my Muslim friend. He wished me a happy New Year and I wished him a happy Ramadan. This evening I went to Shabbat services and the Rabbi's sermon was on the Israeli-Arab conflict. I can't ignore this.

During my time at Camp Simcha I came to revere everyone there for being tremendously ethical, embracing people. I think I called the community "tight-knit" before, but that does not do it justice. There was a caring all around me such as I have never

---

known. However, I came to the poignant discovery that this abounding humanitarianism was, in some ways, rather limited. The orthodox Jews there tended to be vehemently pro-Israel and most of them were rather open about their anti-Arabic sentiments.

These orthodox Jews live together in clustered neighborhoods in America's great metropolises, like New York and L.A. They go to school with Jews, they socialize with Jews, their pediatricians and florists are Jewish. One of the great benefits of being a student at Cranbrook is that I am exposed to international boarding students. My family hosted a guy named Moin and I have become good friends with a boy in my grade, Mohsin. They are both from Saudi Arabia. The people at Camp Simcha have probably never met an Arab, and if they have, were probably so blinded by their preconceived opinions that they couldn't see what I have seen. I have found that these fellow bi-pedal hominids are not monsters: they are gracious human beings (!) who love their families. Indeed, most of the Japanese soldiers in WWII were just shooting at our guys because that's the only way they could get back to their wives and kids. It's easy to depersonalize those who are different from ourselves, but there is a profound beauty and simplicity to the notion that we are, no matter how different, all human beings.

President Bush incessantly uses the term, The Enemy. Calling the Geneva Convention's ban on outrages upon personal dignity vague and "open to interpretation," last Friday, he urged the US Senate Armed Services Committee to pass a bill lowering the standard for treatment of prisoners of war, saying, "The Enemy wants to attack us again." We are led by fear mongers.

We have much in common with "the Enemy". Paramount, we all love our families very much and everything we do stems from a frantic clawing at security for our loved ones in a world where nothing is certain. It is perhaps the only universal human commonality. Even the mothers who strap bombs to their children believe that by blowing up their child and killing Jews, Allah will bring their child into heaven. I'm not pro-Israel and I'm not pro-Arab. I'm pro-peace. So to everybody, shalom aleichem / a salaam Aleichem. The former is Hebrew and the latter Arabic but they both mean the same thing: may peace be upon you."

As he commenced his senior year of high school at Cranbrook, Miles had five new teachers. He acquired a sixth teacher from National Public Radio: Leroy Sievers, a journalist and fellow cancer sufferer. Leroy, who'd wandered the globe as a war correspondent, had been executive producer of "Nightline" with Ted Koppel. He brought his blunt style of journalism to his own fight with colon cancer. Miles derived much inspiration and courage from Sievers, and when Sievers wrote that he couldn't decide whether he would live long enough to warrant the purchase of a new pair of shoes, Miles wrote that he had a similar thought when it came time to renew a subscription to "Wired" magazine.

Miles was himself stepping into the role of teacher as he realized that he was facing a challenge as menacing and gruesome as any that came mankind's way. On October 12, 2006 he wrote:

> When I've had a particularly good off-week, I am filled with a serene resolution and sense of peace. Like I know what I've got to do. It won't be fun, but dying is a lot worse. Bite the bullet; to fret is moot. People ask me how I can keep reliving the most unpleasant experience of my life thus far every three weeks. It's hard, but that's how.
>
> I am spurred to ride into the face of the storm by the knowledge that I have wholeheartedly enjoyed my time in the sun. Sometimes, as toxicity fades, I'll just sit in a chair, doing nothing in particular except basking in the feeling of health itself.
>
> Though the prospect of two weeks of daily vomiting and unrelenting nausea is daunting, I have savored my reprieve. And that gives me strength.

He knew that his family and community were feeling real hurt and sorrow for him. On October 17, 2006, typing through severe nausea, he wrote a poignant update which was eventually carried internationally by CNN, the Cable News Network:

> "Wow, I'm so sorry you have to go through this, Miles. What can I do to help?" I get this all the time. (A perfect response, by the way.) And frankly, I've struggled to supply an answer. Invent a cure, that's what you can do. I've wished, hitherto vainly, that I could give people something small, something realistic yet

meaningful, which they could do to help and support me. In its own way, I'm sure it has been as hard (harder?) on the people in my life who have had to pace the sidelines powerlessly while I suffer. However, considering the degree of nausea through which I am fighting to type these sentences, I'm having a hard time believing it at the moment. At any rate, if you've taken the time to read my postings, you're probably hurting too, so here is what you can do to help:

Read my CarePage. I don't update that often and I put a lot of effort into making them worthwhile....Your following my progress and sending thoughts of healing in my direction are the quickest, easiest ways of supporting me. 2) Donate blood. Last year I personally needed blood and many of you stepped up to the plate. The chemotherapy temporarily shuts down the body's blood producing factories in the bone marrow, making blood transfusions of vital importance. With the treatment I am currently receiving, blood production dips, but so far not dangerously so, meaning I have not needed transfusions. But it's not just about Miles. You can literally save somebody's life in an hour. What could be more worthwhile?

3) Grow. There's nothing you can do for me. You can tell me you're sorry, but you can't make the cancer go away. What you can do is let yourself be changed, in any number of ways, by my struggle. A college friend decided to try and quit cigarettes, citing me as one of the inspirations. Personal action means the most to me. Realize what a wonder it is to be healthy and alive. Appreciate (and employ!) the power of a kind word or deed. Be there for somebody else when they are going through hard times---this is the real measure of friendship.

If my struggle with cancer galvanizes actions of goodness, I can rest assured that even if I succumb to the rogue cells, I will leave behind a legacy of victory. Dying is not what scares me; it's dying having had no impact. I know a lot of eyes are watching me suffer; and---win or lose---this is my time for impact. If all is naught but random atoms in the void, then that would explain a lot, like Darfur and why I wound up with alveolar rhabdomyosarcoma; but if there be a purpose, then this is my hour. I have tried my best to show what it is to persevere, and what it means to be strong.

The school year was unfolding nicely, all things considered. By mid-October Miles had learned that he had indeed been chosen as the Cranbrook homecoming king. Also, with Dr. Wexler's approval, a home-visit nurse, Tina Leitch, began to administer Miles' chemo in the comfort of our home. Just prior to Halloween, Nancy and Miles flew to New York for an evaluation by Dr. Wexler. A PET scan was performed and the results were ambiguous. A spot was detected in the left shoulder. There was a need to consult with a senior radiologist to see if a biopsy might be necessary. Dr. Wexler, dressed in a Halloween Batman costume, sent Nancy and Miles back to the Ronald McDonald House to await a decision. Nancy went back to the room, opened up the laptop computer, and wrote this update:

October31, 2006

And now the mom weighs in.

When Batman, aka Dr. Wexler, informed us that the results were less than the hoped for all clear, and recommended that we return home this evening as planned, I remained cool, calm, and collected. Miles later told me that he was surprised by my reaction, or lack of, and commented that I have changed. It's true. Cancer changes a person......in mostly good ways. A person is forced to develop humility, compassion, patience, and gratitude. It's about muscles. Miles' cancer is about muscles. I have new muscles, and the one I'm speaking of now is the capacity to tolerate ambiguity and uncertainty. I've known for months now that this ride is a roller coaster. Ups and downs, ups and downs. Mostly downs. Last night, following our Japanese dinner, I had the best sleep I've had in a year and a half. Didn't know then that we would hear the dreaded, 'there's something suspicious on the scan', but then again, I wasn't totally surprised. As Miles pointed out though, I'm different. I've matured in more ways than I ever would have imagined or thought possible, at least at this moment. I've learned to take it as it comes. I've learned that nothing is for sure until it's for sure. I've learned to expect nothing and be grateful for everything. I've learned that this journey will test us at every turn. I know that we have done everything humanly possible to increase Miles' chances of survival. I know that we are in good hands - the best. When the going gets rough, you want strong fighters on your team; and I've got them. I'm poised on the head of a pin, a razor's edge, the twilight zone. It would be arrogant to say that I know he'll be fine; I know no such thing. It would be equally false to conclude that our months of chemo were for naught. I'm living in uncertainty, pure uncertainty. And the truth is I've been living there since the afternoon of June 4, 2005. The jury is out. Sometimes the jury comes back quickly; sometimes it takes days. But, like waiting for the verdict, it's out of my hands. For some reason, I'm more at peace with that reality than I have been since we started our fight. We live scan to scan: that's our life now. We better enjoy it; we don't know what tomorrow will bring.

What tomorrow brought was this: the physicians' best judgments were that the spot detected by the MRI was unlikely to represent a metastasis. Miles was also approved for a final round of chemo, representing the last bullet in Dr. Wexler's gun. Going off chemo made us nervous because 80% of Stage 4 kids relapse and, of those who do, half relapse around a year and a half after diagnosis. Miles was just a couple of months short of that point. Despite the anxiety of being weaponless, Miles seemed to have reached a point of joyful transcendence. His updates at this time reminded me of Lance Armstrong's expression of gratitude to cancer for giving rise to such positive growth in his own character, for causing him to appreciate so much about life on the planet. As we approached the 2006 Thanksgiving holiday Miles wrote a double-header on November 22 and 23:

November 22, 2006

Here are some bits and pieces of writing I've jotted down over the past two weeks or so. It hit me midway through my morning drive from Beaumont hospital to school. It hit me like an opiate: the world was as bright and crisp as I could ever recall it being. My calendar is on November, but no, there is something... supernatural...going on here. Science could not justify this meteorological fluke. There was not a cloud in the sky. I rolled down my window and stuck out my hand. The wind rushed cool through the seams of my fingers; sunshine warmed the back of my hand. Indian summer was heaving a last, splendorous breath. I realized, in waves, a series of ideas that seemed worth writing down. Already late for class, I continued to drive with one hand, while simultaneously writing on a little piece of paper pressed up to the steering wheel. It was by no means safe. Had I crashed and died, mid-epiphany, after having been the recipient of close to a million dollars in medical care…I don't even know. I couldn't find a way to put the writing into one concise update, but I'll say this one thing: I don't know what's in my future, relapse or cure, but I may be in that last glorious day in Fall, and it may go very wintry after that. But if, God forbid, cancer cells do resurface, it's not going to be tomorrow, or next week—that much is pretty certain. I have time. And you can bet I'm savoring it. It's a strange feeling to have that awareness at age eighteen, but such a blessing too. If I could elect to get cancer with all the risks and benefits, I think I would. I probably wouldn't pick rhabdo though, if I were allowed to choose. Hmm. Even if it had to be rhabdo, it'd still be a close call. But just the fact that I might volunteer for this ordeal is really saying something about the upsides of personal struggle.

The U.S. population hit 300 million last month. Cases of rhabdomyosarcoma in America annually: 350. How wild is that?! (On top of that, my presentation is extremely rare.) In such a situation there is only one thing to do: buy lottery tickets. I bought my first one last weekend. I'll probably win. Here's another little statistic. 516 days down, 12 to go! We have pushed on with poisoning after poisoning and I am now hitting my physically tolerable maximum. When I'm not doing chemo, as I haven't for the past couple of weeks, I feel normal, though sometimes a little weak. However, my insides are war-torn. My bone marrow is exhausted (though I can't really feel that.) My immune system is wiped out. I would hate to be a cancer cell right about now. My body will almost fully recover with time, although there are some long-lasting side effects.

Three days in to the last round EVER. I got my blood tested on Monday to see if I could handle it—my last chance before the doctors were going to scrap the round—but I made it. I'm glad. As my mom put it, to stop one round shy of completing the course would be like getting disqualified in the last mile of a marathon.

I'm feeling a hearty dose of nausea as I type this. Food odors make me feel worse, so I tend to avoid the kitchen when people are preparing food. I just went down there, though, a second ago, to find the smells of sardines and bleu cheese wafting into my nostrils. That didn't help. Why anyone would willingly ingest bleu cheese (even when they aren't nauseated) is a question which truly baffles me to the core.

November 23, 2006

A CarePage doubleheader here. Bear with me, I must. It's Thanksgiving. If cancer doesn't teach a person how to be thankful for what they have, for each day they are given, then I don't know what will.

I am thankful for the basic necessities that too many in this world do not have: food, water, shelter, clothing, and basic medical care. 1 in 5 Michigan children are living below the poverty line (this is America that we're talking about.

I am thankful for the luxuries, which too often I take for granted: A three-car family, health insurance, education, a country that protects my rights. I realize that in spite of the cancer, I am still infinitely more fortunate than so many.

I am grateful to the blood donors who have sustained me. I am grateful for my family and friends, so many of whom have stuck by me when the going got rough. People worldwide follow every update. People I've never even met are praying for me. My peers, I know you don't always know what to say or how to act, but you are doing great. Just the other day I got a call from a new friend, Danny, who was just calling to make sure my blood tests went ok. Two others, Jenny and Merrill, have insisted upon undertaking an hour of driving to bring me some pie since I'll be spending my Thanksgiving evening getting chemotherapy. I am thankful for kindness. What are you thankful for?

Short of feeling the gratitude I should. There's just so much. A Hebrew prayer is coming to mind which thanks God for making the land different from the sea, for making it firm, as otherwise life would not be possible. So much blessing does not even occur to us.

I do know I am thankful for this last one with all 100 trillion cells of my being: I AM ALIVE. I wish you health, peace, and fulfillment. Have a happy Thanksgiving.

By this time in the course of his illness, Miles had accumulated a few hundred stable, devoted CarePage readers. They responded in force to his question "What are you thankful for?" They were thankful for their health, their good fortune, the love of their families, and so on. Many also wrote to say how thankful and privileged they were to be members of Miles' CarePage community:

"… Just about every posting has brought a choked throat and tears welling."

"… I have been so uplifted by your thoughts."

"… you have taught us how to dig deeper into the reserves of our souls, to find courage and love. It is a rare human being who can transform his or her adversity into a gift for so many."

"Thank you for reminding me that life is wondrous and awesome and ridiculous and precious."

Many readers, who hadn't previously contributed comments, not unkindly termed lurkers, began to come out of the woodwork. A classmate, Kat Davis, wrote:

"I realized that I'm doing nothing to support you and our friendship unless I let you know that I'm here. It's strange, but I've never been able to think of you as 'sick'… to me you have always seemed full of spirit and soul and health. You have one of the greatest minds I have ever encountered and one of the fullest spirits."

Nancy wrote a message to Miles on the public message board. "I feel privileged and honored to be your mother. I will always cherish the path we have walked together, as true companions, developing a relationship of mutual respect and admiration. My love for you is endless and knows no bounds."

I also wrote a message: "You fell sick a lad but have been abruptly and fiercely advanced far into manhood. Still, I cherish the moments when the medical interventions are quieted and there is time for boyishness. I so enjoyed our taking up the game controllers the other night and blasting Rommel's panzer tanks in the north Libyan Desert. Thanks for the lesson. Love and respect, Dad."

Nancy's brother, Wayne, saw the forest, not the trees, and wrote to the entire CarePage community:

"Dear Fellow CarePagers,

So many moving, genuine, important, and heartfelt things have been said on these pages in the last few days, by friends, relatives, and especially Miles and his parents. …We have all gained such insight and perspective through this experience. Throughout, Miles has been a model for us all, setting a tone of optimism, growth, candor, and depth.

Reading all the open, profound, funny, sad, reflective, soul wrenching, elevating comments on this webpage has also forged a sense of community, of belonging, of participating in something precious, even extraordinary, something painful yet enriching, beyond ordinary and commonplace, that continues to give greater meaning to our lives, something that in perhaps another context, somehow might even be considered a ray of the sacred.

I am deeply honored and so grateful to Miles and all of you, each in our own way, to be a small part of this, and feel such warmth through the clouds."

Wayne's review of the impact of this CarePage community on its members was timely in that Miles was just about to complete treatment and, if it was successful, we all might be going each our own way. It would be a sweet parting, for the best of reasons. But for now the CarePage was a platform for Miles to exult in his accomplishment:

December 03, 2006

I'm done. It feels really weird and hard to believe, but I've completed the course. I'm not quite sure what to do with myself now. There's this vacuum---this anti-climax. I don't think it has fully hit yet. For 18 months, completing treatment was all there was. The rest fell to the background, triviality. And so I put foot before foot, onward, vomiting, madly marching towards this paramount goal until suddenly.....It's over. Jolt. Like when you're walking up the stairs in the dark and you get to the top, you lift your leg as if to climb another step, but your foot finds only air beneath it and you start forward.

Treatment has become a way of life. I have found myself unintentionally driving towards the wrong destination---towards Beaumont hospital. Over the past 18 months I've come to know my caregivers so well. I've come to know myself so well. The people you meet along the cancer road are not ordinary people. That goes for patients and practitioners both. I haven't said much about my home care nurse, Tina, but for the last four months of treatment she brought into our household not only biohazardous chemicals but an unbridled enthusiasm which we thrived on. We had a good time, as impossible as that sounds. If cancer-people are ordinary at the outset, that changes pretty quickly. Cancer creates an entirely new person, reorients one's internal compass on the most fundamental level. If I survive, I can safely say it is the best thing that has ever happened to me. Besides being born, I guess. That's definitely up there.

I've played my hand as best I could. My mom threw the deck out the window altogether. I have had more chemotherapy than even the high-risk RMS (rhabdomyosarcoma) kids get at Sloan Kettering (and MSKCC is known for being aggressive). Now it's just a matter of waiting to see what cards the dealer holds. When I told people I had one more round to go, they would exclaim, "Wow that must be such a great feeling!" And it is. It is a better feeling than most could understand. But it's also scary, and I'm not sure people fully understand that. I'm entering a period of peak vulnerability, a rung of the ladder upon which most people slip and fall. I hold my breath and enjoy the shapes in the clouds.

It was as if Miles had been a stone in a great slingshot, stretched to its limit for eighteen months and then released. He was now accelerating forward, soaring. One might say he had completed an advance placement class entitled "From Boyhood to Manhood". His love of life was unbounded. His joy reminded me of the prayer said in Jewish homes each Friday evening to welcome the Sabbath. It is called, "Come, my Beloved" and it includes the following lines of verse:

"Arise, go forth from the ruins; too long have you dwelt in the vale of tears; He will show you abounded mercy. Shake the dust off of yourself, arise, and don your glorious garments - my people.

Arouse yourself, arouse yourself, for your light has come; arise, shine. Awake, awake, utter a song; the glory of the Lord is revealed upon you. Come, my beloved, to meet the Bride; let us welcome the Sabbath."

Miles called it "Life from concentrate". His joy gushed from the CarePages:

December 09, 2006

I can't tell you how much I am enjoying life right now. This is it, friends, right here. And there is a chance, although not a particularly high one, that with the conclusion of chemotherapy I have closed the cancer chapter and I'm on to the next one. Cancer is never totally in the past...I will get CT scans every couple months for the rest of my life, but it is possible that my deepest fear is spurious. Maximize each day. And if the cancer cells are already multiplying once more, this is doubly pertinent. I often come back to the thought: I am living incomparably more richly than I ever was before cancer, so if I die, will it have been worth it just to get these couple years of super living? Ultimately no, I suppose. But will I have had more positive impact on the world (the main component in my definition of success) having gotten cancer and died versus having lived an ordinary life? That is to say, would it be better to have lived as a sun, which, at an early stage, supernova-d fleetingly, giving everyone in his life a lesson in rolling with the punches before fading, or to be an ordinary star amongst billions in the galaxy? We'll never know for sure, but I think about it a lot.

If I am to survive, I can't help but quiver with an indomitable sense that the pieces are falling into place to construct something special. Hopefully I'm not being supercilious when I say this. "

Miles did not delay for a moment in applying himself to the construction of something special. Just six days out from eighteen months of chemo, he placed himself on the standby testing list for the "ACT" college admission test. He skipped a day of school to spend seven hours diving into test preparation material. The next morning, he took the test and afterward wrote in a December 9, 2006 CarePage update, "… this morning I gave it my best. I've never focused so hard for so long. I wanted this so badly… I have an underlying need to prove that I am still normal."

The following week he flew to New York for scans and was delighted to report that they were "clean." But he worried that his return to normal health might mean losing his CarePage readership:

With each clean scan, my chance of survival gets better and better. Therefore, each clean scan engenders the best news I have ever received in my life. And that's going to take awhile to sink in. I have three months to bask in it before the next set of scans in March.

Some of you have inquired about the future of CarePages. They're not going anywhere. My goal is to update about (and at least) once a week. I selfishly hope you'll stick around; I don't think people fully understand what a source of strength it is to go on this site when I'm feeling overwhelmed and read a handful of your well-wishes or anecdotes. To all my dedicated readers, thank you again for your continued support.

Actually, instead of Miles losing his CarePage readers, his CarePage readers lost him. He was so delighted to be free of medical exams and treatment, so enraptured with prosaic living, that he was nowhere to be found as far as his readership was concerned. Nancy stepped into the breach:

January 19, 2007

Unlike the previous times in which I posted because Miles was too sick, this entry by me is to let you know that Miles is alive and well and his dance card is full, very full. Miles has crammed more life - normal life - into the last four weeks than he has in the past 20 months. The good (the best) report of clean scans in mid December launched a full program of making up for lost time. The winter break was filled with an overdue family vacation, first to central Florida, a less frequented area, and then a cruise to the Bahamas. Just prior to departure, Miles and Jon renewed their scuba certification and enjoyed an underwater excursion during the cruise. The entire family partook in a snorkeling adventure (even the mom) which was a highlight - especially the immersion in a school of breathtakingly beautiful and colorful fish. Miles will provide a report of his experiences and impressions when he comes up for air. At the moment, he is knee-deep in final exams, college applications, and SAT's. Not surprising, his essays involve reflections on his cancer experience; they are extremely thoughtful and inspiring. He's beginning to embrace his identity as a cancer survivor, though he doesn't know yet exactly what that will mean. He is keenly aware that his destiny has been shaped by this experience and it carries a responsibility.

He looks terrific: he has a full head of hair albeit short, he's put on a few pounds, he's managing a full schedule, but mostly he's high on life.

That's the way it should be at age 18 and a senior. He's ready to leave the nest; he's ready to fly. Nancy

It wasn't until late January that Miles came around to giving what he called "A report from the New World." The exponential growth in his self-awareness, worldliness, and sensitivity to others was readily apparent. It made me so grateful to have him involved with our community and so proud to see how carefully he did so:

January 27, 2007

A report from the new world. I've been meaning to do an update for awhile, but have been unsure of what to say. It's come to me now though. Just what words shall fill this space, I'm not sure, but I felt the call and I have come in answer.

As the distance between today and The Cancer Months continues to grow, I look back on them with an increasing sense of disbelief. While it was happening, my eyes were pressed up so close to the pages of the novel that, thankfully, I couldn't make out the words. Proper perspective would have been crippling, inducing a permanent state of catatonic terror. Now though, as I draw back, the text sharpens into focus and I stare in amazement at the plot of my own biography.

Eight weeks out of treatment now and already I know (as if I didn't before) that my life will never revert to what it used to be. I'm feeling the late effects of chemo and radiation: the fatigue, the periodic resurgence of nausea, the mental fuzziness. Still I fall under the 'relatively unscathed' category. Some people who underwent what I got are now in wheelchairs due to nerve damage. And yet, in some ways, life right now is strangely and completely normal. I have resumed a full course load for the final semester, which includes some very interesting electives: Writing Workshop, Human Geography (an interesting socio-political-economic-geographical-cultural study), Existential Hero (not quite sure what it's about yet, and already I have the sense that I will never fully be able to explain).

My ethereal cancer aura has ebbed a little (the return of eyelashes helps), and I find myself twisting and looping around that godforsaken rollercoaster of Raging High School Puberty Land once more. One foot is still in the cancer world, mind you. We've had some little scares...weird pains, odd scan results. It comes with the territory. If your throat is sore, you reason you're probably coming down with a cold. If my throat is sore, we can't help but worry that maybe some of those cancerous lymph nodes went unradiated.

Living in two worlds is nothing new to me. So then what is new? Well for starters, I'm taking glassblowing lessons. The studio is in this ancient warehouse in Detroit. From the outside you would think it's been abandoned, but inside it is filled with rising artists looking for cheap space. I'm there four hours every Sunday, wielding long pipes of molten glass. Hmm, that makes me sound much more skilled than I actually am. It's really hard. I'm getting better though; I made a quality beer mug last session. It wouldn't sell on the shelves of IKEA, but hey, it's complete with a handle and I made it myself. My next session is tomorrow.

Last night I went to a warming house and handed out hand warmers. I went with my girlfriend, a couple of our friends, and a Cranbrook English teacher. The warming house opens at about 8:30 every night, but a small band of chilly people congregate outside the doors long before that. So we went to try and warm some hands and spirits while they waited. I talked with several people, and man, what an eye-opener it was. Most of them have lived elsewhere -- Florida beaches were a common theme -- but have somehow been carried forth by the unguided currents of day-to-day necessity, winding up here, on a cold winter's night in Royal Oak, Michigan. Most of them did not have Oliver Twist childhoods. One man told me of his comfortable upbringing, living in big house complete with a swimming pool in some Southern state, I forget which. Somehow he tripped and hit the ground hard. Yet the thing that struck me most was how cordial everyone was. An adventitious family has formed amongst these people -- this community. Everyone shook hands, asked how each other how they were getting by, shared a cigarette. One woman, who had recently broken her ankle but did not have any access to medical care, went up to a man, hugged him and said quietly, "I love you." Standing there in that dark parking lot with toes numb, I was touched. As I left, I thought of something I've written before: It takes the darkest, bleakest of human tribulations to bring out the best in us.

Siting here, cozy on my living room couch with my cat, writing and listening to Bob Dylan's new album, I think I finally understand how Hunter S. Thompson felt as he wrote these words: "I returned to the Holiday Inn — where they have a swimming pool and air-conditioned rooms — to consider the paradox of a nation that has given so much to those who preach the glories of rugged individualism from the security of countless corporate sinecures, and so little to that diminishing band of yesterday's refugees who still practice it, day by day, in a tough, rootless and sometimes witless style that most of us have long since been weaned away from."

And you can't help but see those individuals, homeless yet at home, and think what a bittersweet world this is.

No news was good news for the next four weeks as Miles continued to savor every moment of his life. And then, one morning in mid-February, his circumstances became more bitter than sweet.

CHAPTER NINE

RECURRENCE

Miles' birthday and mine are exactly six months apart, his on August 25, and mine on February 25. I was about to turn fifty-six and Miles eighteen-and-a-half in February of 2007. We had planned to go out to a nice restaurant on my birthday, but Miles came down with a fever a few days prior. The fever persisted and he was admitted to the Beaumont Hospital pediatric unit. While the infectious disease docs were trying to unravel the cause of the fever, an x-ray of the chest was taken. This gave the doctors a chance to re-measure an enlarged lymph node they'd noticed a few weeks previous. It was determined that the enlarged node had increased further in size. This was bad news. It represented a turnabout in his fortunes. Miles tried to put a positive spin on it for his readers:

Cancer is far short of the only possible cause, so we're trying not to get too far ahead of ourselves. False positives happen all the time in the cancer world, but nevertheless this isn't exactly the kind of news you want to hear. As always, my doctors are on top of the situation and I will be going to New York in two weeks to get a full set of scans (an x-ray is pretty crude, can't draw any firm conclusions from that, save for the unequivocal presence of a non-specific something).

It seems it's always something. Still, this is not the time to panic; that would be premature. But I'd be lying if I said I wasn't scared. ...I cannot begin to describe the terror --- and even if I could you would never comprehend it. But it is what it is, and whatever it is, we'll deal with it. I'll keep you posted.

Feeling fear, admitting fear, and not going into a panic, that takes courage. Indeed, that is courage. Miles' actions and his reflections at this juncture suggest to me that he had already steeled himself for this development. It appears he had begun the grave task of abandoning the perspective that he might outlive this cancer, might go to college, might marry, might have children, and might have grandchildren. He allowed the fear to wash through him and then, on March 10, he posted one of his most sublime, poignant updates:

March 10, 2007 1:00 am EST

The fear is mostly gone now. Even if things don't work out for me in New York, I'm not scared anymore. The way I see it, it's possible that all things are deliberate (though I don't think anyone can know for sure), in which case these past two cancer years may be my reason for being, and if so I give myself an A for how I've handled this harrowing ordeal. If I am no more than a 25 trillion cell organism which unfortunately got the short end of the stick, I have still thoroughly enjoyed the time I've been given. We're not entitled to one breath of air, yet here we find ourselves alive anyway. You didn't do anything to earn it, so whatever you get is bonus.

A lot of cancer victims are angry at life, at God, at the rogue cells within their bodies. I don't have much anger. I'll hear people say things like, "I hope this chemo really hurts the cancer." I always think to myself, no, it doesn't work like that at all. These are not evil entities; there is no awareness on their part (there isn't even a "they"). Cancer is simply a series of cellular processes. It's like if a child drowned in a river and you got mad at the H20 molecules.

I might be more than a little disappointed with the hand I've been dealt, but it is what it is. Thinking about what it could be is pointless. It ought to be different, that's for sure, but it ain't. We deal with realities, not pretty possibilities. And I'm sorry, cancer, but I refuse to stop enjoying life. I made that decision at the outset.

What you'll one day realize (if you haven't already) is that death is not something to fear, it is only something which one must come to understand. Though the prospect seems so hugely incomprehensible, it's really not. It's something that happens, just as anything else happens. The world keeps revolving around the sun, which in turn keeps on hurtling round the Milky Way. On a personal level, it doesn't look to be an unpleasant experience. It's pretty neutral as far as I'm concerned. There is a primordial terror of The Great Unknown, all instincts pitted against it, but these primitive feelings can be transcended. See, things only matter in context. If the universe ceased to exist, it wouldn't matter because there would be nothing there for it to matter to. In the silent contextlessness, everything is alright. Because there's never going to be enough time to do everything you want to do, but the time I've had has been time enough--time enough to make the world a better place for having been here, I like to think, if only in limited circles.

So my pain is not for me; it is for you, my friends and family.

But if by some miracle or struck of luck this is a false alarm, it will be the greatest existential and spiritual call to action I have ever had the misfortune of receiving. I see no way to just set this aside. I have not given up hope in the possibility that I am cancer free; I have simply come to accept either way. Now we find out if I have a flair for high wire escape artistry. I fly to New York on Sunday. It's not clear how long I'll be there, it all depends on what the scans find, but look for an update later in the week. Either way, it's going to be alright.

Tears come to my eyes as I read this passage. I feel so proud of the heights he'd attained at this juncture. Nancy was proud too. She put a message to Miles on the CarePage saying, "You pull me along – often kicking and screaming – into acceptance of what is. Love, your mom and now your student."

From here on out, his climb became even steeper and the elements much more severe. Yet he gave no ground. His clarity and determination seem to have acted as a beacon call to angels. For life began to offer him support in surprising and profound ways. The day that he wrote the update cited above, he had been to Borders Bookstore in Birmingham, Michigan, where he'd seen people in line to have their books autographed by television newsman Bob Woodruff. The next day Miles and Nancy went to Detroit's Metropolitan Airport to catch a flight to New York. As Miles tells it:

March 11, 2007

There is so much in this world that I do not understand.

I was in the security line at the airport with my mom this morning. We looked over, and there was Bob Woodruff, the ABC anchor who had been injured in Iraq. He was with his wife. I had seen him at Borders for a book signing the day before. I hadn't waited in the line or anything, but I saw him nonetheless. Here he was again at the airport. Not only is he a Cranbrook graduate, but he is slated to be our commencement speaker in June. We introduced ourselves to him. He responded compassionately to the nature of my trip, giving me his business card. I told him I was running for student speaker at graduation and that we'd make quite a duo. We went through the metal detectors and separated.

Turns out we were all flying to LaGuardia, but our flight got cancelled on account of engine maintenance, so we were rerouted to Newark. We met up again at the gate. We talked to him and his wife, Lee, for about an hour. He asked for my cell phone number. It turns out we have a lot of common ground, being so acquainted with the medical system, and they seemed to regard us as equals in plight. Mr. Woodruff started to cry at one point and kissed my mom on the hand.

It was an amazing meeting. Our fates seemed intertwined... that I should meet this journalist/tough-it-out extraordinaire who graduated from Cranbrook and we might be co-speakers in June. In the course of my time with him, he appeared on the airport's television news screen in front of us and in the New York Times he showed us. The most powerful thing of all was that they too visibly felt moved by our encounter. And I felt in a way I have no memory of feeling before, the presence of angels in Gate A67. I don't mean Mr. and Mrs. Woodruff, but a guardian presence I could not see. It's a pretty good way to start this trip.

Yes, it was a good start, for Bob and Lee Woodruff proved themselves over the ensuing months to be true, devoted, earnest, and faithful friends to Miles. Miles was about to visit another great friend also, the dedicated and talented Dr. Leonard Wexler. In New York City Miles and Nancy settled in to the Ronald McDonald house and, the next morning, went to Sloan Kettering for fresh scans and blood draws. Another day passed as the results were evaluated by Dr. Wexler. Finally, in the inner sanctum of Dr. Wexler's consultation room, there was somber news to deliver: The cancer had spread and was growing rapidly. Unfortunately, radiation and chemo were no longer viable options, as the radiation field would be too large and his body could not tolerate additional chemo. Dr. Wexler, as doctors will do, sugar-coated the bad news by holding out one ray of hope. He said that a trial of a new drug, an IGF1R-inhibitor, was being carried out at select teaching and research hospitals in New Jersey, Baltimore, and Philadelphia. This drug theoretically interfered with receptors related to insulin growth factors, and prevented Rhabdo from binding to, or exploiting, healthy cells.

I don't believe that Dr. Wexler actually thought that this drug would alter the course of Miles' disease. This experimental drug was in the early trial phases and it was not well understood. Its activity in the body was very complex, involving intricate signaling pathways along long amino acid chains and across specific intermolecular bridges. Furthermore, it was not clear that Miles could be chemo free for a long enough period of time to qualify to join a trial. I believe that Dr. Wexler's aim was simply to keep hope alive. We desperately embraced this glimmer of hope, but there was also, speaking for myself, an element of pretending and avoidance in this embrace. As for Miles, I cannot really say what level of hope he had in being saved by an experimental drug, but he put on the face of one who was not ready to call it quits:

...we've seen the chemotherapy fail now and, in light of that, we feel this new treatment is the best option.

I'm actually doing better than I would have expected, as are my parents I think. Though I didn't say it before, I was pretty sure the cancer was back. I remember how it felt two years ago and it felt the same. Only while I thought I was now out of options, it turns out I may be participating in one of the most exciting new options to come along in years. We are on the move again, and that is empowering.

In short, there is a time when all bullets have been fired and the game is up, but this is not that time. At this point, we find ourselves confronted with a hurdle, not a wall.

A change with respect to our use of CarePages began at this point, a shift in emphasis. Instead of using it largely to report Miles' course of disease and treatment, Nancy began to use it to reflect on our harsh journey and to pay tribute to Miles' conduct and his personal growth in making that journey. Nancy led us off in this new direction on March 14, 2007 when she posted the following:

March14, 2007

The mom here again. The news changes by the hour - never a dull moment- and there have been some developments that Miles will report. I'm writing the human interest story this time. I want to share a bit about my experience from a mom's perspective. Let me first say that my eyes are drinking in, literally soaking up, MILES. I look at him and find that I melt with peace and joy. Though he's cancer filled, he radiates life. He is my boy, but he's not a boy; he's a young man. He started this journey as a kid, but he is clearly his own man now. I know that you know - from his writings- much about his outlook, his skill, and his maturity. I must describe some other qualities about Miles that may not be as readily apparent, but are noteworthy. I think it's important to toot his horn NOW, as we literally do not know what tomorrow will bring.

It is not uncommon for cancer patients/kids to feel that when the treatment fails, i.e. the cancer wins the war, that somehow they weren't a good patient. Illogical but understandable. When we met with the doc on Monday to get the dreadful but expected news, I wanted to say, even before Miles would even think those thoughts, in front of his doc and his father, that Miles was truly extraordinary throughout his cancer treatment in terms of his attitude. Not one complaint. Not one. Ever. No self pity. His acceptance, and with such grace, of his circumstances and his fate was and is saint like. When he's hit in the gut with a bad piece of news, he's down for short period of time, then rises again with his indomitable spirit, and asks: what next? I hear him on the phone relaying horrendous pieces of information, yet he's still right in there fighting.

I swear he doesn't have a mean bone in his body. Throughout this recent ordeal, he stays on top of his friendships, his relationships with family, and most of all, his very important relationship with his beloved. He's beginning to know his impact on others, and he views it as a responsibility. He has impacted his world in more ways than we can know.

I used to think that I had something to do with who he has become, but lately, I think not. He's too incredible to be the work of parenting. I don't think it's his doing either. It is simply who he is and what he is here to do.

I feel tremendously grateful to have had the opportunity to know him, to love him and to be his mother. He wasn't the easiest child to raise, being different from the beginning. I always tried to preserve his uniqueness while at the same time prepare him for the world: The true challenge of parenting. What I see now is that he has changed the world, while being in it in his own way. Mission accomplished.

This new direction in our writing brought new people into our conversation, people who had been lurking. One new mother wrote, "Nancy, I have learned so much about parenting by watching how you and Miles have negotiated this most terrible of terrors together." A woman in her eighties wrote, "I appreciate living as I never have before." An adult cancer survivor wrote, "You are an inspiration, valiant, and a hero in my mind." The mother of a child with cancer wrote, "I read your words and I feel such a sense of peace. Your sharing this journey with such honesty and rawness brings me to value life so much more, appreciate what I have, relish my experiences, and have a loving and grateful perspective on each new day. I imagine it has this effect on anyone who is fortunate enough to read the CarePages." Tina, Miles home chemo nurse wrote, "I feel so enriched having crossed your path." And, Sue Chaplin, a mother of one of Miles' middle school classmates wrote, "I don't think in all my 53 years I have ever known anyone so courageous, so giving, so loving ... No matter what happens you will have affected more people than you could ever imagine. Thank you." Such comments were extremely important to Miles. They were affirmations that he was having an impact. What he did not know was that his impact was soon to be magnified enormously.

CHAPTER TEN

SEARCH FOR A MIRACLE

Miles was not Dr. Wexler's only patient – as a renowned pediatric oncologist, his time was in great demand. Yet he managed to place calls to colleagues and drug researchers in the states of New Jersey, Pennsylvania, Washington, Baltimore, and Detroit to see if there might be room for Miles in one of their drug trials. He also spoke with pharmaceutical companies to see if an exception might be made for Miles to receive an experimental drug under a "compassionate use exception". My cousins, Glenn Cantor and Andy Levin, both of whom worked in the field of pharmaceutical research, also reached out to colleagues in high places.

Finally, on March 15, 2007, Miles was granted a "compassionate use exception" for ImClone's trial of an IGF-1R inhibitor drug, which he would be able to receive at Children's Hospital in Detroit. It is extremely rare for such an exception to be made for a drug which is only in stage one of the four stages of trial. As happy as we were to be granted an exception, it was Dr. Wexler's opinion that Miles' tumor burden would increase too much during the two-week wait before the start of the trial. Since we had already concluded that Miles was finished with chemo and radiation, I felt that he had no choice but to participate in this upcoming drug trial. Although it probably wouldn't save his life, I hoped the experimental drug might buy him more time than would conventional treatment. But Dr. Wexler told us he had been thinking of a regimen, a combination of light radiation and a carefully formulated chemotherapy, that he thought might beat back the current tumor burden and allow Miles to take part in a later trial. It was emotionally exhausting to process our options, but we decided to take Dr. Wexler's advice. After making this momentous decision, Miles, Nancy, and I all posted updates on CarePage. Miles shared his thoughts about very profound matters which might fall under the rubric of applied philosophy:

March 16, 2007

I'd like to do what I can to examine the wrenching existential confusion we're all feeling. What is happening to us calls forth some questions that unfortunately don't have easy answers, as much as we would like them, but here's what I've got so far. It's difficult to comprehend what sort of (fair and merciful) God—if there exists one at all---would do this to Miles Levin. Things can start to look pretty senseless and random. Through this despairing prism, nothing in the world makes any sense. There is no purpose; there is no meaning. Shakespeare said it best: "Out, out, brief candle! Life's but a walking shadow, a poor player that struts and frets his hour upon the stage and then is heard no more: it is a tale told by an idiot, full of sound and fury, signifying nothing."

Frankly, I'm not convinced beyond unconvincing that there is a God. It would make a lot of sense that there wouldn't be, that what has happened to me is no more than a random DNA transcription error, a rearrangement of genes KHR-PAX3 and PAX3-FKHR, which has caused my cells to multiply wildly.

….When told I'd relapsed, I thought to myself, "Two years ago the waves swept me overboard. Why did I keep kicking my feet even as the currents carried me away?" Here I fought as valiantly as I possibly could; I continued to undergo chemotherapy even after the conventional protocol ended, stopping only when my body physically could tolerate no more. We did everything. What do I make of a world in which that's not good enough?

Why didn't I call it a day two years ago and save myself endless vomiting and suffering? Because the only way to know if she will go to Prom with you is to ask her out. Our power is not infinite, and there are times when we will fall short despite all efforts, but the only way to find out is to find out. I have no regrets.

I tend to believe that there is a God. Maybe not a guy with a white beard, but I think I feel the presence of some divine form—I think I feel your prayers—though like the Tao, God could be formless. I have come to believe that God put me on earth to get Stage IV alveolar rhabdomyosarcoma. Why? So that I could show the world how to have Stage IV alveolar rhabdomyosarcoma—or rather how to handle what is close to the worst thing that could possibly happen to me with as much strength and grace as I could manage. I promise to continue to be the best model I can.

The reason I will go through these next few months (or hopefully years and years) and lie on my deathbed with a smile is because I know in my heart now that, as my mom says, "This is who I am and what I am here to do." I know you feel powerless and helpless right now, and would do anything you could to make me better. I want to tell you that watching thousands of you rally behind me has been a validation of success in my worldly mission. The reason I did all that chemo "for nothing" was to let me enjoy the best two years of my life and to fulfill my purpose. Before cancer I was nobody. A nice guy, perhaps, but I didn't have my act together at all, and perhaps never would. Then my hour came, and you have assured me with your words and tears and prayers that I have delivered. In showing me that I have changed many of you profoundly, you have done for me all that I could ever want or need. Thank you.

Nancy wrote about how the news of the recurrence of cancer affected her:

As for me, I want you to know that I, personally, am not devastated by this news. I expected it. I've done too much research to know that Miles' chances of beating this unbelievably aggressive force, given the number of prognostic factors against him, was close to impossible. Unfortunately, though there has been great advances in cancer, especially pediatric cancer, the sad truth is that there has been no, absolutely no, progress in the survival rates of metastatic rhabdomyosarcoma. I did not expect (but suspected) such a quick and destructive return, However my deepest wish is that he is able to avail himself of this new cutting edge treatment.

My second wish is that he continues on this planet until June 8 so that he can attend his graduation, see Bob Woodruff, and hopefully speak to his class. (And that the wonderful folks at Cranbrook are lenient with respect to fulfilling graduation requirements.)

I've had many months to deal with the unthinkable. Of course, the reality is another whole thing, but I've worked at every level to accept reality - for ultimately, there is no choice. I would be less than honest, though, if I didn't say it breaks my heart, constantly and deeply. It's a rare night at our house that I don't check his breathing - and often several times in the wee hours - and heave a sigh of relief when I see that sweet smile (yes, even when he sleeps) and he is inhaling and exhaling. It's a strange world we live in when we're grateful for poison.

It seems that all of you appreciate our updates, and it also gives me a chance to release (win win). My mantra now is something I read: DON'T BELIEVE IN MIRACLES, DEPEND ON THEM.

Nancy

Miles started another chemo round with some new drugs on March 17, and then, in the wee hours of March 18, he went into a medical crisis. The pain was so acute that I thought it might be his final crisis. As Miles tells it:

Around 3 am Friday morning pain abruptly took hold of me until I quickly found myself being assisted through snow into a cab, then in Urgent Care telling the nurse that the morphine wasn't working. The resident on call didn't know what was wrong with me. The pain pierced all over my body. I pulled a 102 fever in a matter of minutes. I was sweating bullets. I was pretty sure that my liver had ruptured and I was going to die within hours. Even so, I felt prepared. I was smiling, just as I said I would be. I knew I had a lot to be proud of. At least this would be swift.

I guess the bad news is that I burned through another one of my nine lives. Fortunately, Dr. Wexler told us the next day, it was just a reaction to the new chemo: fever, shaking, flu-like symptoms, and exaggerated pain at the tumor sites. This is a funny place, and if you ever think you've got it pegged down, you know less now than the day you were born. You may just win the lottery tomorrow; look up at the heavens in thanks, only to notice a huge asteroid scorching across the sky, the earth around you becoming a million seismic shards exploding outwards through space seconds later, all Ferrari dealerships obliterated. Probably not, I suppose, but who's to say? "

When he was stabilized and discharged back to the Ronald McDonald House, Miles wrote an update that was addressed as much to the disease itself as it was to his readers:

76

....I'm not going down to this thing. My physical body may be subject to biological forces beyond my control, but my mentality is not. What happens to my body is insignificant anyway because it is temporal, and even if it breaks, that's not me breaking. The infinite and enduring me is the me as I am remembered. I am not so much the pebble dropping in the pond as I am the ripples that follow.

I'll try and explain why this is the best thing that could happen to me. There is only one path to greatness and it runs through hell. Trials make or break a person. The greater the ordeal, the more strength you'll attain upon surmounting it or the further you will fall. So while I have been given a terrible curse, I have also been given a rare opportunity. I would go so far as to call it an ugly blessing. While it has been challenging, I've had friends, family, and resources to help me through it.

If I had to pick one thing I would hope to accomplish in this life, it would be to show people how to rekindle the human fire from cinder and fading embers until the flames burn so bright that it hurts to look.

I am doing fine because I refuse to do otherwise. That much is mine. Attempts to extinguish my fire thus far have only intensified it. With each crashing wave, I plant my feet deeper in the sand and become more resolute. If my health declines, some may say I "lost" my battle with cancer; but as for me, I can't think of too many ways in which I could have been more victorious. If it comes to it, I'll go down in magnificent flames, purely for the principle glory of the thing. But hopefully it won't come to it. Ishould also say that I've really perked back up a lot over the past two days. I'm several days out from chemo, although I have another round on Wednesday. My cousins came in from Boston for the day and we met some New York Knicks players who were at the Ronald McDonald house to sign autographs. Also my girlfriend and her mom flew in today and I got to see them, which was a definite boost for my spirits. It's really not bad here: I just lay in bed and go on my computer while my mom goes out and gets me ice cream and California rolls. I don't understand what all the fuss is about.

Two comments came in from members of the faculty at Cranbrook Academy, telling Miles that he had been elevated to the status of a teacher.

Miles' football coach, Curtis Williams, posted a comment to Miles for the first time:

"I'm sorry that I have not written before but I wasn't sure what to say. I am always proud of my players in their many endeavors but you take the cake. I know that our time together was short…a few agility drills and a ton of stairs, but I'll be a better coach…strike that…a better person for having met a man of your character and toughness."

The Head of the Upper School, Charles Shaw, wrote on a Friday, just after the students were let out for spring break:

"Time for me to commune with you, Miles. To think about everything I've stored up today from your teachers, administrators, and your friends. Your teachers are pretty much in love with your language now. English teachers try to teach students to write the way you write. Language that is clear, spare, playful, fresh, purged of pretention. It's also the language of Act V. I loved your reference to Macbeth. You're writing from within Act V now. This is where you get to ask all the questions the world greets with impatience and sneering. Why did this happen? What does it mean? Where does the universe end? In great exasperation when I was young, my mother would reach the limit of her patience after my tenth question or so and say 'Charles please don't ask me any of…your…what-if questions." Miles, thanks for helping us to ask the questions again. Thanks for the courage. Thanks for helping me do my hard job. Thanks for making my school better. Thanks for helping my faculty. We love you."

Meanwhile, undergoing Dr. Wexler's customized chemotherapy in New York, Miles was inundated with visits from women. On March 21, he had the company of his mother, his girlfriend Robyn, and Robyn's mother, Laurie. The next day, his Aunt Carolyn, Nancy's sister, visited for a few hours, bringing candy and flowers. The following day, having just finished the Cranbrook Wilderness Expedition to the Smoky Mountains, his sister Nina arrived. She had been met at LaGuardia by representatives of Chai Lifeline, the organization that sponsors the summer camp for kids with cancer, and posted this update:

Chai Lifeline extended their copious support towards us yet again by offering to pick me up at the airport and safely drive me to the Ronald Macdonald house, free of charge of course. My mom greeted me at the door -outside on 73rd street- wearing her nightgown. I hadn't seen her in almost two weeks because of my Wilderness trip. Together we rushed upstairs to see Miles, who was waiting just as eagerly to see us. My first impression was that he looked like Moses, a full faced beard tracing his features. We hugged (of course) and within a few minutes I had thrown on a pair of sweat pants and got in bed for some much needed sibling cuddling. My mom brought us sushi and we picked out movies for this evening. Now I see what he's talking about: this really IS the life.

Of course, there are many obvious things about this situation that are far from desirable. In the many dark hours that I have experienced since my return from the Wilderness adventure, one thing has already become obvious to me: in light of everything, it is crucial to find happiness in the small moments that seem prosaic, without closer inspection. In that moment, lying in bed, eating sushi, and watching videos on YouTube, I realized the true sense of the meaning "don't take things for granted."

Miles, as we can surely understand, began to show fatigue and frustration with his situation. Here it was, late March of 2007, with the tulips getting ready to emerge and his classmates enjoying their Spring Break:

I'm on spring break right now. This is my senior Spring Break, and this is how I'm spending it. While others are tanning on beaches in Mexico, I'm sick in bed. And I've been sick in this same bed, in this same room, for almost two weeks now. Luckily, I'm usually so far beyond feeling sorry for myself at this point. This is mainly because, were I not doing all this chemotherapy that has caused me to miss out on relaxing tropical adventures, my projected date of death was somewhere around…tomorrow. But once in awhile (particularly when I'm sick, cold, tired, and hungry) I feel a little pissed. It's a friendly reminder that I'm still a human, at least for a little longer.

I got back to my room, slumped down on my bed, and checked my email. I was too tired for any kind of splendiferous fulmination, otherwise I would have. Then I read a message from a relatively new friend, Sarah, whom I had recently given my CarePage link. She had just finished reading every single post I'd ever written. Sarah's caring instantly restored me. The support I feel make makes this whole thing so much easier. I ran into a mom I know down at the hospital. Like us, she and her son come from afar to be treated at Sloan, staying here at the RMH at night. She told me that her sister, a minister in Virginia, read my golf balls entry in her sermon (update #9, some of you CarePage old timers may remember it), apologizing if this in any way violated my wishes. On the contrary, I was honored. This is what keeps me going, knowing that my suffering can be transmuted into something that will impact people on a scale much larger than I can know. It's not much of a pleasure being inside my body anymore, and I could stop treatment and let it all be over any time I wish, but these affirmations remind me that my remaining life is now about something bigger than that. I must keep on.

CHAPTER ELEVEN

DISCOURAGEMENT

Having completed his most recent chemo and radiation therapies in New York, Miles and his mother flew back to Detroit a few days later. Nancy told CarePage readers that she understood and supported his sense of discouragement:

I've told him that he has every right to be upset, deflated, and downright angry. I've also told him, many times, that he does not, I repeat, he does not need to maintain an upbeat attitude all the time. Enough of the taking care of his friends and families; it's time for him to take care of himself. He sounds heroic, and he is, but he's also in pain. He sounds courageous, and he is, but he is also compromised. He sounds brave, but I would imagine that he is also afraid. The importance of "setting the record straight" became clear to me when I heard Miles tell Dr. Wexler that he felt pretty good. I'm the mom; I see the truth, and the truth is that he doesn't feel pretty good. Nor do we, his family. This report is not to say that we haven't been truthful; we have. But, as you can imagine, there's another life behind closed doors.

Life is tense and uncertain at our house. Miles has symptoms that come and go. We don't know if or to what extent the chemo is working. We're dreading the words, 'he needs another platelet transfusion', which are likely, even this afternoon. He's scheduled for surgery on Thursday – to install a mediport for chemo. We're back in the world of cancer treatment: the thermometer is on the counter; regular trips to the pharmacy and hospital; energy level fluctuates, and most of all, uncertainty.

Miles was concerned that Nancy had given the impression that he was fearful and not being straight with his readership:

Today I had to get another transfusion. After one round of chemo, my counts have plummeted to all-time lows. My platelets are low enough that I am at risk for spontaneous internal bleeding and my immune system is so weak that I could become infected by my own body. And I must wait until my counts come back up before I can start the next round of chemo. The cancer, meanwhile, doesn't. My back is really against the wall now.

On the emotional side of things, I have to disagree with my mom. I resent any implication that my attitude is disingenuous. I said I'm not afraid of dying and I meant what I said. I worry about the misery between now and death, but not the phenomenon itself. My mom and other adults have told me it's ok if I have feelings of fear or anger, as if I'm trying to hide them from everybody. This frustrates me. I know its ok; I just don't usually feel that way.

So although I'm usually positive, I do have my occasional down moments. I assure you I'm not ashamed of them at all. Who wouldn't? But for the most part, so long as I'm not suffering too much physically, I'm happy and strong. However, I don't know anybody who can feel as intensely lousy as I did for days on end and still be eternally upbeat, except maybe Jesus. CarePages is me, though—I don't pretend to be okay when I'm not. Yet it is important, I feel, to provide you with a balanced account of this experience. I sometimes regret not filming these past two years and making a documentary, but I realized today that these CarePages are just another journalistic medium, and my best method of coverage is through my words.

CarePages reached 20,000 visits last week, with over 460 readers (it's an iceberg readership, most have never commented). If you feel inclined to tell someone about our journey, please don't hesitate to do so. You'd be doing me an honor. Most readers are standing just beyond the outer edges of this destructive forest fire, but I can still see the flames glint in so many of your eyes. And those reflections, I think, are the best thing you can do for me.

There was a woman who responded to Miles' call to "tell about our journey". That woman was Laura Berman, a journalist with the *Detroit News*. She and my mother, also a journalist, had been friends and colleagues for many years. My mother had been diagnosed with terminal cancer in early January and was spending her last months in her house in Birmingham, Michigan. Laura was prominent among the friends who paid frequent visits to my mother to keep her company. Although Laura had been a CarePage reader, Miles' situation was made more palpable by her hearing details directly from his grandmother. Laura decided that she wanted to write a column telling her readers about Miles' cancer journey. But when she pitched the idea to her editors, they didn't see the newsworthiness of a story about "another kid with cancer". Laura told her editors about Miles' blog and begged them to take a look at his CarePage. They needed reminding, but eventually they did and were impressed. So much so that they gave her a green light to do the story, including having her travel to New York to visit Miles at the Ronald McDonald House. That a newspaper was interested in doing a story about him came as good news to Miles.

Further good news came on April 1, when Miles learned that he had been accepted to both of the colleges to which he had made application:

> On a bittersweet note, I got into both of the colleges I applied to, Kalamazoo and Oberlin. In my Kalamazoo acceptance letter, the person who reviewed my application called my essay "one of the most beautifully written and powerfully inspiring pieces of writing [he] had read in a long time." I guess that means I did it. I continued coming to school all through treatment, staying on course to graduate with my class, managed respectable test scores without a chance for preparation, and got into college. I was not going to be denied. That much feels sweet. But it's not happening now anyway, certainly not in 2007. At least I can be proud of my efforts. I suppose if I had been rejected it would have just been bitterbitter.

His prestige among his classmates had been growing as more of them had started reading his blog. When he returned to school at the end of Spring Break, he was accorded special attention from both students and staff. Here is his account of arriving at the dining hall at lunchtime:

> I spotted the back of Robyn's red head at the front of the room but it took me like fifteen minutes to make it to her with so many happy stops along the way. It was especially strange to reunite with the student and faculty CarePage readers. Without saying a word, so much was already tacitly understood.
>
> For my only actual class of the day, Existential Hero, my teacher (Eric Lorrey) gave me the whole hour to speak to the class. I wasn't really sure quite what I'd say, but the words found me. At one

point, when I'd asked if there were any questions, someone wanted to know if there was anything I really wanted to do before I die. There are a million things I'd like to do before I die. I'd like to jump from a diving board into a pool of Jell-O and flobble around in the blobbly gelatin. It is just not possible to finish an all-you-can-eat appetizer platter, and house policy prohibits to-go bags on such selections. But to answer the question: while there are plenty of things I'd enjoy doing, there is nothing I feel I *need* to do before I can die peacefully. I've already checked those things off.

To our great despair, however, we were not engaged in an academic exercise. Our boy was dying, and he knew it. After flying to New York with Nancy on April 6, he wrote, with crystal clarity and admirable maturity:

I'm in rough seas now, with a cancer weight clasped around my ankle, pulling me down beneath the waves. I've come close to drowning a couple times, but lately it looks like all this furious kicking might just bring me back to the surface, at least for awhile.

As I've said before, our ideal plan is to use the chemo as a stopgap measure, holding me over until I could switch to the experimental treatment. If there is ever going to be a springboard juncture, we think this is it. I say this in part because my health peaked on Monday; the chemotherapy toxicity had subsided and the cancer growth had been restrained, but the pain resurged Tuesday evening, and I've resumed a rapid decline ever since.

Considering the prospect of starting (the experimental) treatment next Wednesday in Detroit (no constant commuting to Baltimore), having only had to wait 21 days... I burst into the open air and filled my lungs. I'd made it to the surface.

For about thirty seconds, I was treading water. I felt a hope I've not known in weeks. I will always hope for the best, but for a second there it looked like the best might actually happen. Barely outside Wexler's office, we got a call from LoRusso. The study in Detroit is closed. The drug companies are not accruing patients at this time.

This is some rollercoaster ride.

Both Wexler and LoRusso are continuing see what might be available for me. Wexler mentioned something at Vanderbilt, and Baltimore is back on the table. As of an hour ago, he had not yet heard back from either. Considering that an experimental treatment is really my best shot, and as the chemo option isn't all that promising anymore, we are going to hold off on chemotherapy for at least the weekend. I will deteriorate noticeably, but it's now been over two weeks since I've had any treatment, and chemo would restart the clocks.

Hopefully someone will come through. If not, Dr. Wexler is trying to engineer some out-of-the-box treatments that might get me to graduation. We're in a period of uncertainty, which is better than being in a period of certain hopelessness.

How do you know when it's over? When it's over. That may be soon, but it's not now.

Miles' girlfriend Robyn and her mother came to New York to spend time with Miles and give Nancy a break. Nancy could relax with them standing watch, knowing how they loved Miles. Nancy took a little "R and R," ambling about Manhattan on foot, buying a celebrity gossip magazine and watching the passersby. Then she got back to work, feeling her way into the decision about whether to fall back on chemo or fall forward into the experimental drug:

We are at a crossroads. There are so many decisions to make and critical ones at that. Opening one door closes another. Making one choice precludes another. Though we have a wonderful and wise team leader, Dr. Wexler, nevertheless, the decisions are ours; ultimately the decisions are Miles'.

In the crudest sense, the decision is: how much should we allow this cancer to grow wildly, i.e. how much should Miles suffer, before we intervene with chemo, which could provide short term relief but no long term gain?..... How long can Robyn's touch keep the reality at bay? How long can I continue to dance on the head of a pin?

It's about time. It's about buying time, but at what cost?

Ultimately, the decisions are Miles. Yes, we are here to support, advise, clarify, and validate, but ultimately, it is his life on the line and his suffering to endure. Sometimes, he feels up to the task; sometimes, particularly when he is in pain, he is again my child appealing to his mom for comfort and to "make it all better". Never has the saying 'there are no easy answers' been more true. Regret is a toxic emotion. I'm striving to avoid it. However, decisions, choices, paths must be chosen, all with high price tags, all in the context of many unknowns, uncertainties, and hopefully not some inevitabilities.

I will do what I have always done, particularly since June of '05. Incubate. Listen for the voice. Hear what others say, including and mostly Miles' truth. I will incorporate, integrate, but mostly wait, and then, move forward with the wind at my back, knowing that I am at once both leading and being led.

Dr. Wexler ultimately pushed us to a decision by emphasizing that we were placing too much hope in the experimental drug, and underestimating the potential of tools still at our disposal. I believe that Dr. Wexler knew that there was virtually no chance of the experimental drug being effective at this stage, but he held it out to us to foster hope. Seeing how thoroughly we had latched onto that hope, he needed to say something to loosen our irrational grip.

Having made the decision to stay in New York, Miles wrote a sobering update that informed his readers of the choices he faced and the choice he'd made. In this update he coined a phrase which became his mantra – "Keep fighting, but stop struggling":

April 11, 2007

Miles here,, at the hospital. I could not begin to guess how many people are standing behind me in an army of prayer. It is deeply incredible to feel so loved by so many. And hopefully somebody up there will listen to you guys, but it's looking more and more like my future holds other plans. The CT scan revealed that the cancer is making its way to my lungs, one of rhabdo's favorite travel destinations. While the lungs are not currently full of tumors, fluid is beginning to build up in the pleural cavity surrounding the lungs. This has caused me to lose my voice. The other tumors in my body are progressing rapidly as well, as evidenced by the soaring LDH levels.

My mom and I were concerned that Dr. Wexler would tell me that the cancer has spread too far for there to be anything to be gained by more treatment, that the game is up, that it's time to just go home. Fortunately, I still have some options. He presented me with three different chemotherapy combinations. (Waiting out the remaining period of the 28 days is too dangerous). Last night I told

Robyn that I would do at least one round of the most aggressive stuff they'll offer me as an early birthday present to her. Now I'm lined up for a 4 drug, 96 hour infusion, which will keep me in New York for another couple weeks. I have a 1 in 2 chance of responding to this treatment. Let's pray. If I don't respond, there will be no future options. I will be too sick from the cancer by the time I recover from the chemotherapy to do anything about it. To be clear, by undergoing this treatment, I hope only to buy a little more time.

As Dr. Wexler presented me with the option to discontinue treatment, I thought of you. I pledged that if it came to it, I would go down in magnificent flames for the principle glory of the thing. This treatment may result in nothing more than causing me additional unpleasantness for the last two or three weeks of my life, but my strife continues. I want to show everyone how it's done. You don't stop fighting until it's over. Meanwhile, we must be realistic in our understanding that while this isn't over yet, it looks to be soon. Thus, my mantra has become: "Keep fighting, but stop struggling."

CHAPTER TWELVE

ACKNOWLEDGMENT

On April 17, 2007, Miles wrote "The Disappointment Essay," in which he began to look at his life retrospectively – acknowledging pain, sadness, and disappointment:

I'm only going to say this once.

Part of the power of CarePages, I've been told, is that it resonates a certain authenticity, free from pretense. But I'm sure many of you must wonder sometimes, "Wait, how could he not be upset about what's happening to him?" Without pretense and sugar coating, I now say, no, this not what I had planned.

First I should address the anger issue. That's the easy one because, as I've said, I really don't have much anger. I don't. I have moments, but for the most part I accept this. I have done everything I can to try and survive. If it is to be, it is to be. As for "Why me?"... I don't know, and I've given up wondering. If I have a divine purpose, it is to show the world how to deal with adversity head on, with courage and grace. If I am saved by science or chance, I still showed the world how to deal with adversity head on, with courage and grace.

I come back to the analogy of the baby drowning in the river and getting angry at the H20 molecules. I'm not angry because there's nothing to be angry at. Anger requires a target. You have to be angry AT something. There is no target; there are only abnormal cellular processes.

So I'm not angry. This is how it is. But I am so terribly sorry that this is how it has to be. I so badly want to live. I have great enthusiasm for life; that probably shows. This is the first CarePage update I've ever written through tears. I just want to live. NPR Columnist and cancer patient Leroy Sievers says it best for me: "I'm not scared to die, I'm just not ready.

It was hard for me at school when all my friends got worked up about the colleges they had not yet heard back from. So much talk about college. It was hard to hear. Firstly, all that stressing about which Ivy League they'd be going to while I'm stressing about whether those suspicious scans meant cancer and The End or not; and secondly, that everyone would be moving on to the next stage of life...the whole College Experience...onwards to young rising professionals and newlyweds and fathers and mothers and grandfathers and grandmothers and retirees...but my life ends here; this is my stop, a couple months short of graduating high school. The truncation is so harsh. That's what hurts the most. There's so much more I want to do. And I know I have more to give. I got the short end of the stick, and while I'm not angry (at a stick?), I'm painfully saddened and disappointed. My own life is the most tragic thing I have ever known. How many people can say that free of melodrama?

I try to hold in mind that all you can do is work with what you're given, and I pretty much made the most of it. I'm proud of that. Whether you live to be 18 or 81, your tenure on this earth is still fleeting. For the happy and healthy, it will always be too short. Given this, all you can do is do some good, I suppose, and find a couple things to laugh at in between. I've done that.

Most of the time I'm not sad. When I feel well, I'm happy. But when I'm feeling happy and well is when I realize how much I enjoy this whole thing, how much I'll miss it (although I don't think I will be capable of missing it once I'm gone)–and that's when I have the hardest time letting go. This is, as I titled it, The Disappointment Essay. I've always appreciated a quote on the way things are by Hunter S. Thompson. "It's a strange world," he wrote, "Some people get rich, others eat shit and die. Who knows?" That seems about it. And who knows?

Who knows? I believe through cancer I was able to rise, coming respectably close to self-actualization. Maybe I never would have gotten my act together otherwise. Into adulthood, I might have been scattered, eternally five minutes late to life. Maybe this has put my good where it will do the most. I can only hope so.

Every untimely death has a tragic component which draws our attention. In November of 2009, our local newspaper carried a story about a southeast Michigan boy who died at age five, a victim of a multi-year struggle with neuroblastoma. Noah Biorkman was his name. Knowing that he was unlikely to see another Christmas, friends of his family started a campaign which resulted in Noah receiving more than one million Christmas cards. Because of his age,

Noah's dilemma had a certain purity and simplicity, which in no way reduced his family's pain in losing him, but perhaps clarified the sentiments of the people who sent him a card – sympathy and sadness.

There was a complexity to Miles' situation that caused people to identify with differing facets of his personality and soul as he formed evolving points of view. They met him as a distracted, unfocused, privileged boy of sixteen when he began writing his CarePage updates. They watched as he journeyed to the threshold of manhood. He was about to turn nineteen. His wings were dry. He was able to express himself in honest, rich language. As his Cranbrook writing teacher, David Watson, put it:

"His point of view came out of his own fire. He somehow had the strength, and grace, to laugh in the shadow of his possible and then probable, and then inevitable annihilation, to see himself clearly, and to see through all the easy truisms we tell ourselves about such matters because we cannot face them directly. This made his writing authentic and strong. His story was life – life struggling as it must to continue, to flower, to express itself fully."

Miles became many things to many people. Responding individually to whatever it was that moved them, his readers came out in droves:

A physician wrote, "I have never encountered a patient with your level of understanding of the complexities of illness. You have taken hold of my heart."

A teacher of writing wrote, "I almost can't believe that even now you think so naturally of giving rather than taking….your generosity in a situation that certainly justifies selfishness is staggering."

A cancer patient wrote, "I want you to know that you help me immeasurably when I go for my treatments. You give me additional strength to go forward."

A rabbi wrote, "The depth of your sharing from your heart is the caring gift you have given each of us."

Another teacher wrote, "You have taught me more about becoming a human being than anyone I know."

A Sufi wrote, "You have been a vehicle for love in this world, you touch so many with your struggle, your pain, your hope, and your wisdom."

A woman identifying herself as a lesbian wrote, "My partner and I read what you write together. We are both so touched by your journey. Thank you for helping me live my life so much more fully."

An artist wrote, "You are helping transform matter into spirit, into beauty, light, and truth."

And a person using the name "LA Brown" wrote, "The only time I have shed tears for a stranger was on 9/11...Today I find myself typing through tears for a brave stranger I will never meet...I am so utterly touched, and in total awe of you."

On April 18, 2007 it became my moment to write of shedding tears:

Dear Miles,

I've been retracing in my mind our shared path, which I have been so privileged to share with you. One such recollection pertained to the part of our Omaha period when you were around four years old. With Nancy's attention newly directed to baby Nina, the adventure-providing father replaced the nurturing, warm mother as the focus of your attention. Although you wanted very much to be with me, on most mornings I would have already gone to work by the time you awoke. When I would return from work you would want to "show and tell" all that you had learned that day. You might have taken me by the hand and escorted me to a rock you had overturned earlier in the day, where you had seen a centipede. You might have drawn a picture of a steam shovel, and wanted to describe its workings to me. You might have wanted me to read a story to you from a book. Although there were often many other things to be done between my coming home from work and going to bed, I tried to respond to your interests. But if my attention was not focused, if I was thinking of those other things to be done, you noticed. Two times a minute you might check to see where my eyes were focused and you would nudge me if I was looking away from the object of your fascination. I will admit to you that I did at times have my mind and attention on other things when you did not want it split so. I apologize for that Miles. I remember one particular summer day during that period. On that day you awoke before I had left for work. You were following me around the house, talking to me while I shaved, watching me tie my tie, asking me questions while I made some tea and toast. When it came time for me to leave the house and get into the car and drive to work, you were entirely opposed to my doing so. As far as you were concerned, you and I had begun to play, which meant to your young mind and heart that I was to be your playmate for that entire good, long summer day. When it became apparent that I was leaving you at home, disappearing from your sight, you became inconsolable. You were crying and pressing your tear-streaked face against the screen of the door as I walked down the driveway to my car. I imagine you thinking and feeling in that moment "I don't want you to leave daddy....why are you going away?" In your non-linear mind there was no consoling expectation of my return. Ultimately, your mother found it necessary to constrain you. I remember, as I drove to work, feeling sad and wishing that I did not have to leave you so abruptly. But that was not the way of our world. I was not a farmer whom you could follow to the fields on our back forty or a craftsman with a shop just down the street. I was an office worker who did obscure things in a remote location. I was expected at work and could not tarry to stay your tears.

Now, ironically, the tables are turned. It is you who must compress many tasks into so little time. It is you walking down the driveway. And it is I with the tear-streaked face pressed up against the screen of the door, crying for you to not leave.

I am, as we pray for a complete recovery to be sent from Heaven, watching you my son. My attention is not divided. And I am so very proud of everything you have learned and put into practice. You do us nothing but honor. Love, Dad.

We were all praying for a recovery, but indications were that the train was not headed for the station of our choice. Banba Donnelly – a Cranbrook mom, former nurse, and good friend of ours – put the situation into clear focus without metaphor, allegory, allusion, or illusion:

"Dearest Miles, it seems abundantly clear that you are very, very ill. Your recent postings now talk about death as an imminent thing. If this is indeed the case then I am glad you are talking about it....I hope you realize that in your short life you have touched a great number of people in an astonishing way and influenced so many. You have lived a good and meaningful life. ...you will not soon be forgotten."

Nancy herself contributed an update that had a retrospective quality:

> I think I can say with a high degree of certainty that Miles would not be where he is today had we not developed the relationship we have. Not many mothers, or fathers, have the opportunity of relating intimately with a near grown son, of getting to know at a deep level and being known at a deep level, their teenager. Most kids at this age and stage are out and about, chomping at the bit, ready to leave the nest. …We have worked cooperatively and become a true team. There is mutual respect, admiration, acceptance, and deep love between us. We have faced frightening, overwhelming, and terrifying hurdles and decisions. We have celebrated and grieved together. We have laughed, kidded, shared at a deep level and bonded into eternity.
>
> I have come to know – and love – the person, the soul, the essence of Miles. His depth is staggering. His capacity to understand the human experience has touched me in ways I didn't know were possible. We have become true friends. If I could, I would, in a heartbeat, trade the richness of our relationship for this to be a bad dream. If I could, I would trade this wise, kind, sweet, boy for my disorganized, ADHD, not five minutes but at least ten minutes late kid. But, this choice is not given me. So, I fill myself with the blessings that I have gained by walking this treacherous path with my child, watching him evolve from a boy to a young man, supporting him as he faces issues that no 18 year old should face. I have felt every feeling in the rainbow over the past 2 years – many of them sweet, delicious, rare, and true treasures.

Miles, unfortunately, was feeling some of the most acute pain of his entire journey. On the evening of April 19, in New York, he started feeling a worsening chest and shoulder pain that quickly escalated to the point where an Emergency Room admission was necessary. At Sloan-Kettering's ER, morphine was administered to little affect, other than to make him vomit. It wasn't until two in the morning that the use of Dilaudid brought the pain under control. Miles knew it was show time. When he reported on this incident in a CarePage update, he said, "Watch and I will show you how to truck through some hard stuff."

Just at the moment when he was facing the hard stuff, Miles received word that the following Monday's *Detroit News* would carry Laura Berman's story about him, including the publishing of excerpts from his CarePage blog on the website edition of the *Detroit News*. We had no idea just how much his reach was about to be extended, his impact magnified.

CHAPTER THIRTEEN

FULFILLMENT

On April 23, 2007, the *Detroit News* carried Laura Berman's story about Miles on the front page, above the fold, three columns wide. The headline read, "Sharing His Life – hundreds log on to teen's blog as he battles cancer". Below the headline was a photo of Miles lying in bed at the New York City Ronald McDonald House, his laptop resting on his stomach as he composed an update. Under the photo, in italics, the following quote was excerpted from his CarePage blog. "Dying is not what scares me; it's dying having had no impact. I know a lot of eyes are watching me suffer and – win or lose – this is my time for impact."

The story carried over to fill the entire fifth page, with additional photos and quotations from his updates. Some of the lovely things Laura wrote included the following excerpts.

"...Levin has documented cancer's assault on his body with clarity of voice and purpose that astonishes a growing cult of readers at his Beaumont Hospital blog....reporting with precision and dignity on his treatment, his disease, and his emotions."

"Levin matters to his classmates because he's drilled down and focused the moments on what matters since his diagnosis. He is, as Charles Shaw, head of Cranbrook's upper school describes him, a real-life example of ideas that otherwise come alive only on movie screens for most of his teenage peers. Words like courage, bravery, and hero: 'They see these qualities in Miles.'"

"As I write this, I don't know how many days Levin has to live. Eight days ago, struggling to overcome pain and to speak sitting up, he said he had strived for saintliness, because he had seen how much his own courage inspired and affected others.... Levin has reached for – and seized – the hearts of those around him....In the end he finds himself not alone, he says, but enveloped in love."

Upon reading the article, Miles wrote in an update:

> This article is touching…..This is, I guess, what I've been trying to do. I can only guess because I'm not really sure what I'm trying to do. Despite all the times I've been called a teacher, I have no lesson plan. I just try to live as bravely as I can and that will count for whatever it counts for.

The article had an enormous, immediate, global impact. Anticipating a substantial response, we had set up a new and separate CarePage, called "Levinstory" instead of the original CarePage "Levinmiles." The name of the new and separate CarePage was published in Laura's article. People in South America, particularly Brazil, and in Europe, Asia and other parts of the world were going to the "Levinstory" CarePage. In their comments, many people said they spent hours reading nearly two years of updates from beginning to end.

Miles received an invitation to be interviewed on a popular talk show on Detroit radio's WJR, Paul W. Smith's "Morning Show." Meanwhile, Carol Costello, a reporter at the Cable News Network (CNN) in New York, had read the *Detroit News* article and brought it to the attention of Rose Arce, a senior producer. After Rose read the article, she sent an e-mail to Miles asking for an interview. Miles reaction –

> God is being a pretty good agent in working the media. All I know is that this is the ultimate realization of all I've been trying to do: to inspire as many people as I possibly can with what looks to be the very short time I'm being given. That is my life's purpose, and these are the days of fulfillment. The coverage, combined with my recent improvement in health…..this might just be a bona fide miracle. Starting with the front page story, this has been an outrageously good day. Maybe that prayer surge by the hundreds who participated in the vigil had a delayed effect…. I just had one of the best days of my life.

The return to health to which he referred was the fact that his neutrophil counts were rising again, nudging him toward eligibility for another round of chemo.

At about that same time, a CarePage reader in Coral Gables, Florida, sent word to Miles that, in his weakened and vulnerable condition, he shouldn't have to endure the distressing effort and dirty grind of boarding a commercial aircraft. She and her husband, Riki and Jerome Shaw, insisted that they be allowed to provide a private jet from Teterboro Airport in New Jersey. They also wanted to provide a limousine to take Miles and Nancy from the Ronald McDonald House to Teterboro. Seeing this as all of a piece, and floored by their generosity and sensitivity, we accepted their wonderful offer without hesitation.

Miles and Nancy flew home on the private jet, arriving at Oakland County Airport in Pontiac, Michigan on April 25, a lovely spring day. A CNN cameraman, Jamie, accompanied them. I met their plane as it taxied up to the small terminal building. Not surprisingly, Miles looked very pale and weak as he disembarked. Nancy later told me it was a flight of silence, a couple hours of deep contemplation for them both. Jamie left us to arrange for his rental car. I drove Nancy and Miles home without much fanfare. A little lift was received at our driveway when we saw that our neighbors, Dave and Debi Morgan, had taped a large welcome banner to our garage doors. Miles was not heard from by CarePage readers for nearly a week until he posted this update:

April 30, 2007 at 09:35 PM EDT

I know, I know. It's been six days. Three of those days were some of the busiest—and certainly some of the biggest—of my life. Many of you already know why. I came home last week on a private jet. Readers, I've been spoiled. That was all it took to instill an intolerance of coach class that will never abate. I tell you that's the life for me. No parking garages, no security lines, no lost baggage, no waiting on the runway, good food — pure luxury. It's all thanks to the generosity of some friends who know better than most of us that love reigns supreme. And whatever happens, at least I've got the private plane ride under my belt I guess I can't go any further without letting you in on my little secret. I've just finished three days of filming with CNN for a segment to be aired (possibly next week) on Anderson Cooper 360. My friends at school now know this, as the cameras followed me there, but I couldn't tell anyone at first because I planned to show up at school totally unannounced, and I couldn't spoil the reaction.

My homecoming worked out perfectly as all my friends were gathered together for a senior breakfast. It didn't take long for the large group to realize I was somewhere amongst them. I was bombarded with hugs. It was both strange and wonderful to be back at school. On the last day I was there before I left for New York, I was silently skeptical that I'd ever see my friends again. As my condition worsened in New York, I became surer that that day had been goodbye. Yet there I was once again, against all odds, walking to class, seeing friends, eating lunch, being a teenager.

For awhile, I was skeptical of miracles, reasoning that it has to happen to someone, wondering if maybe a miracle is really only a beautifully improbable occurrence. But when so many variables come together as they have to form the best possible situation (given the confines of reality), maybe that's a miracle.

Not only did I surprise my friends, but they had a big surprise for me as well. Two wonderful girls (Sarah Twedt and Elyse Cantor), have been collecting letters written to me by hundreds of students and compiled them into a book (entitled The Miles Project). I've only been able to do a precursory glance at random pages, but the loving consideration, fondness, and humor are already apparent. This would be a lot harder without friends as good as these. I should also say here that we made a visit to U of M Medical Center. We met with one of the foremost sarcoma experts and he affirmed what we already knew. The experimental treatment holds unparalleled promise, but the drug won't be available to patients until around August. Hopefully I will be able to hold out, but that's a long time.

I started another round of chemo tonight. So far, I don't feel too bad, but this chemo drips in over 96 hours (whereas the common infusion last about an hour or two), so the nausea takes awhile to build up.

It's hard to return to chemo, to being weak and nauseated on my couch when everyone else is having fun and the weather is so gorgeous. It's ok though. Yesterday I spent the whole day with Robyn---a brief but wonderful escape from my overwhelming world. And when being alive during those rare good moments is such a pleasure, returning to chemo seems a little fairer, or at least more tolerable. Even though it is a big step down, I'm also aware that it is another big step towards more of those treasured moments

The ninety-six-hour outpatient infusion was immediately followed by a twenty-four-hour inpatient infusion at Beaumont Hospital – for a total of five days of chemo in a row. Dr. Wexler was scheduling everything with an eye to having Miles be free of all treatment during the days surrounding his high school graduation ceremony in early June. Miles was to represent his class at the ceremony, alongside alumnus Bob Woodruff, the guest speaker. Nancy was with Miles at the conclusion of the five days of treatment. Not wanting him to exert himself any more than necessary, Nancy suggested he sit outdoors on a bench in the sunshine while she retrieved the car from the hospital parking deck. While sitting there, I believe Miles was visited by a mélange of thoughts, emotions and spirit forces which induced nothing less than a state of glory. He understood that he was alive to witness a beautiful Michigan spring day, suffused with promise. He knew that, with twenty-one months of chemotherapy behind him, he would not be seeing another infusion bag for two weeks. Miles realized that his goal of completing high school and serving as an esteemed representative of his class was within reach. He was eagerly anticipating CNN's cablecast of his story. Later he tried to describe his experience:

It's quite something to be propelled out of one of the most hellish days of your life right into one of the most glorious. What comes to mind is this ride, The Power Tower, at an amusement park in Ohio. You've been waiting in the oppressive heat for hours, but then your time comes and this thing blasts you 240 feet in the air faster than you can blink—giggling euphoria in your stomach as the wind rushes through your hair (...once upon a time...) on your way to the top of the world.

As I was sitting outside on a bench (for the first time in a week) while my mom got the car from the hospital parking lot, something special happened. Suddenly, the world (picturesque Beaumont Hospital) became more beautiful than I could ever recall seeing it. There's a certain time at dusk when the sun sometimes sets everything aglow in a most angelic, hyper-real way. Think of the perfect sunset wedding lighting. The splendor of world was overwhelming. As we drove up Woodward, which isn't lined by much more than strip malls, its beauty nearly moved me to tears. I can't remember when being alive ever felt so good, and everything

> around me—the trees, the people in their cars—they were so vibrant with life as well.

This glorious perspective did not immediately dissipate. The next day Miles had to return to Beaumont for an outpatient blood draw. He drove himself there:

> I ventured back into the world today. And even though I was driving to a childhood cancer waiting room, I was in my car with the windows down and my music up and I tell you the honey tastes so much sweeter if you've been stung half to death trying to get it. After my blood check, I went over to Cranbrook and lay in the grass with some of my friends. Then I met up with Robyn and we got ice cream and sat in the sun. One side-effect of the chemo is that it deforms all flavors into a chemical abomination of whatever they are supposed to taste like, but I just don't think it gets much better than that. (Also-Bob Woodruff called me today!)

On May 9, 2007, CNN put Miles' story on the "Anderson Cooper 360" section of their website, with a tab marked "360 Blog: Whatever Life We Get is Bonus". This was CNN's way of building viewership for the airing of the story on that evening's "Anderson Copper 360" show. Within hours we began to receive CarePage comments from new readers who were logging into the "Levinstory" CarePage. People of all ages, occupations, and countries of origin were writing to tell Miles how impressed they were by the way he could write and the way he was meeting the challenge of a killer cancer.

An English lecturer at the University of Nebraska at Lincoln wrote, "You've done more in your short life than many do by the time they are 100."

An attorney wrote, "Your words are reaching many people and changing lives. You've just changed mine."

A Hispanic woman in Texas, whose child died at five weeks of age, wrote "Thank you Miles. You put the faith in life back into my heart."

A medical doctor in Canada wrote, "I want you to know that you have truly touched me tonight."

Muslims and Jews, the old and the young, the sick and the well, the rich and the poor were reading Miles' story and logging on to CarePages to respond, to thank, and to encourage him. Some said they had printed out all of his updates to share with their friends and families. Some said they were at work when they read his blog but could not attend to their work after doing so. Miles felt a great sense of satisfaction and let his readers know how rewarding this was for him:

May 11, 2007

How does it feel to be famous? Everybody wants to know. My reply comes in the form of a smile and a shrug. I'm not famous. Brad Pitt is famous. I walked through the mall today and nobody began to point and squeal, "Look Josie, there's the cancer boy! Let's go touch his head!"

Even so, as I reflected on this recent publicity explosion during my walk to the Apple Store, I still felt just about as perplexed as if a delighted Josie really did come up and feel my head. The general notion that I have cancer continues to be the most unbelievable thing I've ever heard, to say nothing of the response it has engendered.

I remember a couple weeks ago peeking in on the first classroom I ever set foot in at Cranbrook, and I remember remembering the scattered boy that sat in the back row. If anyone had described to him the path that would bring him to me, back outside Room 203, he would have laughed or called the police.

This must be how the Wright Brothers felt as they watched the nose of their laboriously perfected contraption finally start tilting backwards and then witnessing the entire behemoth actually start levitating off the ground, rising higher and higher above Kitty Hawk. I'm sure that somewhere swirling beneath their excitement, Wilbur and Orville simply could not believe it was finally actually happening. They had actually invented a flying machine, and there it was before them, floating weightlessly like gravity had given up. And I suppose it's a funny thing that such experiences are hard to believe, for if they didn't believe it could actually happen, why did they persist through endless tinkering anyway? I consider my own situation. This is more or less what I was trying to do. I was striving to show as many people as I possibly could how to do this as best I can. So now it's actually happening.

The important question is not how does it feel to be famous, but how does it feel to witness the successful actualization of your life's purpose? Certainly, if I am to survive, I've got a few more things I'd like to contribute. But the bitter reality holds this as highly improbable. As such, I must (at least partially) frame my life with smaller borders. I can't plan on much. But in light of the stunning proliferation of my story, I'm starting to feel a little more confident that the essential brushstrokes have made it onto the canvas. In my short time here I've accomplished something respectable. Maybe not enough to bring total acceptance of death, but enough to die with pride.

It doesn't look like it's stopping here either. On Monday, I will be the guest on an hour long radio program called Anything Is Possible, which features a person who has overcome hardship through positive attitude. Tuesday we are heading back to New York for a brief medical check in with Dr. Wexler, as well as possibly filming with ABC (NY local) and seeing our friends at CNN Studios.

I will close this update with something I wrote on October 17, 2006....

"If my struggle with cancer galvanizes actions of goodness, I can rest assured that even if I succumb to the rogue cells, I will leave behind a legacy of victory. Dying is not what scares me; it's dying having had no impact. I know a lot of eyes are watching me suffer; and---win or lose---this is my time for impact. If all is naught but random atoms in the void, then that would explain a lot, like Darfur and why I wound up with alveolar rhabdomyosarcoma; but if there be a purpose, then this is my hour. I have tried my best to show what it is to persevere, and what it means to be strong."

Those words are something different now. They came true.

CHAPTER FOURTEEN

AFFIRMATION

The messages to Miles poured into his "LevinStory" CarePage from all over the planet. The servers at the CarePage office in Chicago were congested with activity. Miles' CarePage had become the largest and most active CarePage ever created. The thing he desired most – to know that he had converted his "ugly blessing" into something positive for others – had been affirmed. The messages were lovely:

"I write to you with moist eyes and from thousands of miles away in India....."

"Your story moved me to tears......"

"Your story touched my heart......"

"You've changed me......."

"I read about you on CNN and have since consumed every word you have written....."

"I saw you on CNN and ran to your CarePage. Read it from start to finish..."

"Because of you I didn't get a thing done this morning...."

"Last night I kissed my kids a little longer, I hugged my stepson harder...."

"We are your ripples and we go forth in honor of you....."

"My breath has been swept away....we have been touched by an angel..."

"You give people like me a reason to pause...I have a new respect for life..."

"You have improved me immeasurably....I thank you from the very core of my being."

Some of the messages fell into certain categories such as "Only Jesus can save you," or urging us to try a miracle cure, a special extract of one sort or another. Many messages of encouragement came from cancer survivors. There were also messages from people of all ages who were dealing with cancer or some other disease. There were many messages from parents of children with cancer or other diseases. But of all the more than ten thousand messages we received, one of the most memorable came to us from a family that had started reading Miles' CarePage in April, when Laura Berman's story about Miles was published in the *Detroit News*. This message came to us from Jennifer, a mother in Ann Arbor, Michigan. It underscored how Miles had impacted one particular person:

"Dear Mr. and Mrs. Levin, Miles, and Nina:

I cannot thank you enough for your beautiful, honest, and heartfelt writing – before and after you even knew that you had the world as an audience. My daughter Lauren, a senior in high school in Ann Arbor, was diagnosed with an inoperable brain tumor 7 months ago. Our family read your story in the Detroit News in April, and since that time, my husband and I, and our son, have read and found comfort and understanding in all of your postings.

I would often find Lauren reading and re-reading your writing. I know she found peace in doing so. On Wednesday, we watched your story on CNN as a family. Lauren passed away early on Friday morning, but we believe she found acceptance through your messages.

There are no words to express our gratitude towards you. You are truly a gift to this world and our family feels blessed to have found yours. Our thoughts and prayers are with you always."

The image of this frail angel looking into a computer screen and drawing true succor from Miles' words, girding herself for the crossing of the threshold by taking inspiration from a slightly older boy, is solemnly beautiful. If any single image represents Miles' wish to have an impact, this is it for me. Jennifer, I thank you for posting that CarePage message about your daughter.

As Miles had noted, a person undergoing chemotherapy has a normal life only during one out of every three weeks. Week one is treatment, week two is recovery, and week three is relatively normal. Miles once wrote that the third week was "what I live for." Dr. Wexler was sensitive to this cycle and he was carefully orchestrating treatment so that Miles' "normal" week would coincide with his graduation on June 6. The week of May 12, 2007, beginning with Mothers' Day on Sunday, was the last "normal" week prior to graduation. Miles received a blood transfusion Sunday evening at Beaumont so that his platelet levels would allow him to fly to New York the following day. On the way to the airport on Monday, I took

Miles to the studios of WJR Radio in Detroit, where he gave an hour-long interview for Jack Krasula's show called "Anything is Possible". On Tuesday, he underwent some tests at Sloan-Kettering and visited Dr. Wexler late that afternoon to learn the results. It was good news, as he reported in this update:

> Blood tests showed that my natural blood production is revving back up again, so I'm on schedule for the next round. I'm withstanding treatment better than [Dr. Wexler] could have or would have predicted. On top of that, the LDH--a protein marker which serves as an indicator of tumor burden--has fallen to 215. Normal is 200. At its highest, my LDH was over six times normal. On top of that, x-rays showed visible reduction in the largest tumor, a lymph node in my chest. I will be getting a full set of scans after this next round.
>
> My foreseeable future has turned from "will he be alive in two weeks?" into "what might he be doing in the fall?" I'm at a loss to explain this turnaround. It must have been that vigil. A month ago my doctor told me he would try his best to get me to my graduation in June, but that he could make no guarantees. Graduating and then dying was a goal. I turn 19 in August, and today it looks like there's a decent chance I'll be here to blow out the candles.

The next day in New York City was, in Miles' words, "busy beyond belief." He gave an interview to the local ABC television station. After that, he had a tour of CNN's studios, conducted by his story's producer, Rose Arce. Rose saw to it that Miles was given some time alone with Anderson Cooper. Anderson took Miles into his office and showed him some personal mementos acquired during his world travels, and then Anderson gave Miles a copy of his book inscribed "With much respect and admiration, Anderson Cooper." After the CNN visit, Miles and Nancy were whisked across town for a high-level reception and presentation on Sloan-Kettering's latest cancer research initiatives. Miles was approached numerous times at the event by Sloan-Kettering physicians, researchers, and administrators who wanted to meet him. Miles had no great appetite for fame, but he did enjoy knowing that he had succeeded in raising the level of awareness of a rare, deadly pediatric cancer, rhabdomyosarcoma. While enjoying the VIP treatment, he wasn't able to forget that he was a cancer patient and that chemo hell waited in the wings. After returning to Detroit from New York, he wrote:

> I'm back at home now, and dreaded Monday is approaching too fast. I want to pause time, but with all the good that's happened lately, I say to the Cosmic Juror: I still think you could go a little easier on me with the chemotherapy, but I agree to your terms.

Our beloved home therapy nurse, Tina, literally saddled Miles with a backpack which contained an infusion pump and chemo drugs. Nancy then wrote an update to sum up the New York experience:

> **May22,2007**
>
> It's about stamina. From the Mom.
> The news from New York was, obviously, fantastic, but for me it was more of a relief. We're still in the game. It's not over. The fat lady isn't singing; she may be humming, but she isn't singing. I never go too far from the hub: I don't get too excited; I don't get too down. This is a marathon, and this is a roller coaster. I take seriously the counsel of Lao Tzu: HOLD FAST TO THE CENTER. Can't spend all my energy on one uncertainty. The cancer ride is fraught with setbacks and small victories. They are a given. It's not that they don't mean anything; it is that they don't mean everything.
> One thing I learned in New York during our last visit is that the ride up the road apiece is uncertain. I say: as long as he is still on the planet, and as long as there are options (and there are, but we don't know what they are) there is hope. I knew that we were in capable hands with Dr. Wexler, but now what we need - and have - are creative hands. We're headed into uncharted territory, making it up as we go...discovering new recipes...adding a little of this (chemo) and perhaps a little of that (some yet to be discovered ingredient). In the meantime I'm enjoying the scenery. It occurred to me last night, as I accompanied Miles while he struggled to pry himself from the couch and lift himself and his heavy backpack filled with fluids and chemo up the stairs to his bed, that this has been a long road, a very long road. We're approaching our two year anniversary next week. With the exception of a three month break (of so called remission)

Miles has been a steady customer of chemo. That takes stamina. How he, and I for that matter, and Jon, and Nina, continues, I really don't know. I could say, and do, "what's the choice?", but there is one. Not that it's appealing, but there is one. I don't think I fully recognized Miles' strength until last night. His humor, his insight, his outlook, and of course his writing skill have become apparent, but I hadn't appreciated his strength until last night. Fighting cancer takes brute strength, endurance, and guts.

On May 25, 2007 my mother died. A non-smoker, she had been stricken by a lung cancer that had metastasized to the brain. I had visited her for a few hours on the afternoon before she passed but, not imagining her to be that close to death, had gone home. I lived five miles away. At approximately 2:00 a.m., the hospice nurse awakened my sister and told her that my mother was failing quickly. My sister called me and I bolted over to the house, but was too late. She died with my sister and the hospice nurse at her side. I was sorry I hadn't been there, regretting that I'd returned home. Learning of her death, Miles posted an update which included this paragraph:

I'm not sure if there will be an update in the next few days. For the past seven months my grandma has been fighting her own battle against lung cancer, and that battle (somewhat to our relief as she is no longer suffering) is now over. She showed me how to continue to live life on her terms--even with cancer, even near the end.

My mother's funeral service had a profound effect on Miles. He witnessed a death impacting a close-knit community. I think he found comfort in the tenderness surrounding the event – the service and the eulogizing, the burial, the sitting Shiva, the condolence calls. An endearing eulogy was written by Laura Berman for the *Detroit News*. My mother's death was not untimely. She was eighty-two-years-old. I believe that being part of this natural lifecycle episode prompted Miles to understand that an untimely death was more difficult for the surviving loved ones. In his update of May 30, 2007, before returning to New York for an examination, he wrote:

Over this past week in spring, there have been moments where I have relished so sweetly the glory of the day that I wish I could encapsulate them in some sort of magic vial to carry into the future. I suppose that's what memories are. I'm back into hyper-living -- the overpoweringly sensitive and exquisite experience of *Now* as very beautiful yet tragically fleeting--but unfortunately, it's for the wrong reason.

In some ways I have the easy role. If I die, I don't have to deal with my loss. Those still here do. It's only when I think of the pain that will sear through my family (and I include Robyn under that heading) that I find this horror more than I can bear. I sometimes try to imagine what it would be like if I had to sit in the audience and watch this happen to Nina or Robyn. The word that comes to mind is excruciating.

Hope is faith in the possibility that something good may happen. In going to New York, we find ourselves very much in that position. There is hope.

Miles revealed to his readers that he had been very depressed in May as he heard his classmates discuss their plans for the future. On June 2, he admitted to his depression and described how he managed to overcome it:

There was a recent period a couple weeks ago where I was really struggling with the fact that all my friends and my girlfriend get to go off to college in the fall with the future in their laps while I get left behind to stay at home doing chemotherapy treatment, if I'm even alive to do that. All those friends who were once my community, who kept me plugged into some sort of normal life, will be far away and very busy. I will fade and I will be bored. That was and still is hard. I know I should feel grateful just to be alive in the fall, but somehow that didn't help. Is it so much to ask that I too could have college to look forward to instead of either more treatment or death?

This got to me in a way that many things in life should be getting to me but I've refused to let them, and that's been the magic of this story. I don't think I did very many updates during this time because I didn't feel I had anything to write that was worthy to read anymore, or of 12,000 people's time. Whatever I had---wisdom or poise or centeredness or whatever--I felt I'd lost. Whereas previously, Miles had been on top of his cancer, now my cancer was on top of me.

This went on for about two weeks before one day I decided that it was enough; I needed some time to deal with that disappointment, but it's enough now and further moping would be a waste of very precious time. I decided that today was the beginning of a change in my attitude, a change in me. I said it aloud. And what I want to tell you in this update is that it worked. I'm back. I feel back on top of the cancer, and will be to the end.

I conclude from this successful transformation in outlook that, to a large extent, a person can make the conscious decision to change their attitude--much more so than I previously thought. It's not effortless; it definitely takes a certain enduring conviction..... But I want to tell you that it's possible.

CHAPTER FIFTEEN

CELEBRATION

Right from the start, June of 2007 was a month of spectacular weather – gentle breezes and temperatures in the mid-seventies. Above were blue skies, at times punctuated by beefy cumulus clouds, with lush vegetation below. All in all, a perfect backdrop was provided for the Cranbrook Kingswood graduation activities. Miles had made it to high school graduation and was to be his class commencement speaker alongside Bob Woodruff.

It was a graduation tradition to have a picture-taking session with one's closest schoolmates. In the late afternoon, before the senior prom, Miles and his friends met in the rose garden of the Cranbrook House mansion for photographs. Nancy and I were there along with other proud parents. Because senior producers at CNN had authorized Rose Arce to cover Miles' graduation, he was being followed around by a CNN camera crew. I had arrived by bicycle and a memorable photo was taken of Miles walking up a pathway to the garden, with me rolling along next to him astride my bike (see photo gallery at levinstory.com). After the photo session, during which I was tearful, the kids walked to the Cranbrook Art Museum where a stretch limousine was waiting to take them to the prom. Nancy described her feelings and spoke for both of us.

June 06, 2007

THE SEND-OFF - TO PROM - FROM THE SIDELINES:

From the Mom.

There were many signs that pointed to good fortune: The message from the nuclear medicine doctor (the docs that interpret PET Scans) asking what miracle drug Miles is taking; the weather today which was spectacular, one of the three days in the year that makes living in Michigan worthwhile; and the fragrance of youth, possibility, and achievement that was emitted from the group of seniors dressed to the nines.

In March, we didn't know if he'd make it to graduation. In June, he was walking, talking, smiling, and ready to dance the night away. He looked fabulous in his brand new Hugo Boss black suit, which had been altered to fit his slim body. As luck would have it (or as Dr. Wexler devised it) he was in his "off" week, so no nausea to contend with and no low blood counts requiring transfusions. The tie was a double Windsor. The shoes actually fit. He didn't have to worry about his hairstyle - no choice but to sport the bald look. Fortunately, bald looks good on Miles. I know I'm his mom and a bit biased, but there's something extremely compelling about Miles, and the bald only adds to it. He looks a bit like someone from another world, and I'm convinced he is.

Robyn deserves her own paragraph. She is the picture of the classic Irish maiden - in color, in appearance, and in core strength. Her beauty is obvious, but it's her enduring devotion to Miles that has won my heart. She can't be more than 100 lbs soaking wet, as they say, but she's Miles' rock, tried and true. The mutual admiration and fondness that flows between them is the stuff that true love is made of. Whatever happens for the two of them, the bar has been set, and it's high.

So, how did I feel, standing there watching my son, and friends, drive off in the limousine for a night of fun, excitement, and abandon? I don't know; I just don't know. I don't have words that capture my feelings about the uncertainty of his future made more acute when juxtaposed against the last twelve years of school and the last two years of cancer treatment. I know I'm proud. I know I'm happy that he gets to experience the incomparable sweetness of prom. I know I'm touched that he has had the experience of young love. I know I'm grateful that modern medicine, through poisoning, has kept him alive. I know I'm scared for my boy. But what I know the most is that I'm appreciative that he has found himself, his true self, and he has that to guide his way wherever that leads. What more could a parent want?

Nancy was reflecting on the blessing part of Miles' "ugly blessing." She was taking pride in what our son had done and who he had become. He had locked eyes with death and not blinked. Miles had done everything demanded of him with the greatest imaginable generosity, grace and determination. He was graduating not just from high school, but from boyhood – into the complete ownership and the full exercise of a virtuous manhood. I, too, was so proud.

After the prom, Miles and his gang spent the night outdoors in sleeping bags in one of Cranbrook's ball fields. He remembered to set the alarm on his mobile phone in order to wake in time for a live telephone interview with Paul W. Smith at the WJR radio studio. After that, he came home and slept the day away. In the evening we attended the Senior Awards Ceremony where Miles received a Booth [Cranbrook's founding family] Citation for an exceptional sense of responsibility and unusual contribution to the school. He also received a Strickland Creative Writing Award. Robyn received recognition as a cum laude graduate. More tears of pride poured into our handkerchiefs.

Friday, June 8, was graduation day. Christ Church Cranbrook, an Episcopal church dating back to 1928, is the traditional site for Cranbrook graduation ceremonies. Unfortunately, it isn't large enough to accommodate the entire graduating class and their families at one time. This limitation was solved by graduating the boys and girls in separate ceremonies on the same day – boys in the morning, girls in the afternoon. The ceremonies had separate commencement and guest speakers. Miles was designated to be the commencement speaker for his class, with Bob Woodruff as the guest speaker. They were told they each would have approximately seven minutes to speak; Miles would go first. The day was to start with a press conference attended by both sets of students, the guest speakers, and by the leaders of the Cranbrook Educational Community. It was covered by local media outlets as well as CNN.

That morning, after dressing for the occasion, Nancy, Nina, Miles and I took some photos in our front yard. The weather was glorious, the sky cloudless and the sun bright. We set off for the church in two cars. After parking, we were directed to a grassy area where photographers were taking pictures of the day's VIPs. Miles was warmly greeted by Bob Woodruff, who asked Miles to please call him Bob, not Mr. Woodruff. Charles "Charlie" Shaw, Head of school, was also on hand as one of the day's dignitaries. We – about thirty people – then adjourned to a small chapel where the VIPs took questions from the media. About ten minutes into the session, Charlie Shaw interrupted the press conference to say that there was a surprise in the wings for Miles. He nodded in the direction of the chapel entry and we turned our heads to find that Dr. Wexler had arrived. Dr. Leonard Wexler, one of the busiest physicians in all of New York, had taken a 5:45 a.m. flight to Detroit in order to witness Miles' graduation. The four of us Levins bolted from our seats and went to welcome him with handshakes and hugs. A lump formed in my throat. There were some questions from the press for Dr. Wexler, which he kindly dismissed, saying that he was just a guest at the event.

Before long we ascended the steps to the main sanctuary for the commencement ceremony. During the press conference, the sanctuary had filled completely with students and spectators. Fortunately, a bench had been roped off for those who had been at the press conference. But, because Dr. Wexler hadn't been expected, I could see that our pew would not accommodate everyone in our party. I insisted that Dr. Wexler sit with my family and set off to find a seat for myself. The only seat available was directly behind a large column which completely cut off my view of the dais. I could hear, but not see, the ceremony. As the opening chord issued from the organ, I took the seat, wondering what I might do about not being able to see my son speak. There was no room to stand where I wouldn't be blocking someone's view. Suddenly I felt a tap on my shoulder. A gentleman leaned down and asked me if I was Miles Levin's father. I said that I was and he introduced himself as Ray Santerini, a Cranbrook alumnus. He told me a section of seats was reserved for alumni and he wished for me to take his seat so that I could have an unobstructed view. I started to decline his offer, but before I finished he drew me up by the arm, saying, "Mr. Levin, please say no more. I insist." With profound gratitude for his sensitivity and generosity, I took his seat just as the guests were asked to rise for the invocation by the chaplain, David Tidwell. Mr. Tidwell said a prayer and read William Blake's poem, "Jerusalem".

Immediately after the invocation, the audience was asked to be seated and a signal was given to Miles to come to the podium. As he left his seat among the students and made his way to the front, his classmates were solemnly quiet. Miles unfolded his speech and set it on the podium. He leaned in close to the microphone because his voice had acquired a whisper-like quality as a side effect of his treatment. I will excerpt a few key parts here:

"Good morning. Before I begin, I just want to tell you, with all the sincerity I have, that I am truly honored to be your student speaker. And also, I can't believe I'm standing here, partially because high school went by so fast, but mainly because I'm still alive at my high school graduation, and for me, that's saying something.

Life is a slot machine. We are here on this earth having been thrust into a random situation we did nothing to deserve, surrounded by circumstances we cannot control. Sometimes chance is kind to us; sometimes we get the short end of the stick. I think the hardest pill we'll ever have to swallow is getting less than we deserve. It stems from expecting life to be fair. We want it to be fair. We want so badly for it to be fair. It should be. It deserves to be. On a very deep level, we need it to be. But it's not. And whenever we fume over some injustice that has befallen us, and when wise friends remind us that life isn't fair, we have to admit with a note of existential resignation that they have a point; but somehow that doesn't really help at all....I can fulminate, I can vociferate, I can raise my banner in protest of everything that isn't fair, but the universe is as the universe does. A pregnant woman will die in a car accident today, and I cannot change that in the slightest.

What feels so deeply wrong about an unfair world such as ours is that it is unfair in a way that, by definition, doesn't make any sense – at least not to me. Some people own private jets, others don't have access to fresh water. I don't get it.

So what I ask you is this: If you are born rich with blessings, if good luck offers you a taxi while an old man stands in the rain, if you are given the seldom talked about long end of the stick, do you have an inherent obligation to use your gifts, resources, and abilities in a sharing and philanthropic manner? I ask you, does having good fortune come with the uninvited responsibility that we give some of it back to the less fortunate?

We cannot be blamed for the things we cannot control, but that does not excuse us from taking charge of the things we can. And while we cannot be blamed for the blessings we cannot control, that does not excuse us from, at the very least, appreciating them. Often, people who have been in peril but escape unscathed, while others weren't so lucky, experience something called 'survivor guilt'. I've never liked the term. I much prefer survivor responsibility. Survivor responsibility carries no guilt, although a moral duty may accompany the blessedness of your life.

You'll have to look inward to see exactly what this responsibility means to you. I can't tell you the answer, and even if I could, I hope I'd be wise enough not to. I will say that all of us here could have been born into poverty or oppression...yet we weren't. And I haven't the faintest clue why. As far as I can tell, it was not merit's hand that rolled the dice. I don't think of myself as a better person than he who goes hungry. I don't think of you as better people than she who gets sick. But for some reason, we have been placed into a world of comfort and opportunity, while others starve and die.

In the end, how much responsibility this puts on you to make something of yourself is a matter of opinion. I can tell you no absolute truth; only ask with all my heart that you consider what advantages we have been given as recipients of a Cranbrook education, and what duties come with this privilege as you head off to your colleges and on into your futures. Please think about it. Thank you."

There was strong, appreciative applause for Miles as he took his seat. Then the choir began singing. During their song I thought about how Miles had said "as you head off to your futures," not "as we head off to our futures." I was proud and bereft in the same moment. After the choir finished, Jim Pickett, Dean of Faculty, introduced Bob Woodruff. He told the audience Woodruff was a graduate of Cranbrook's Class of 1979, that he'd worked on the school newspaper, the "Crane Clarion", had played soccer, and was co-captain of the ski and lacrosse teams. In 1983, he'd obtained a bachelor's degree from Colgate College and, in 1987, a Juris Doctor from the law school at the University of Michigan. Bob was in China teaching law when CBS hired him as a translator for their coverage of the Tiananmen Square uprising in 1989. Subsequently he joined the ABC Network and rose through the ranks to head their Chicago bureau. He lead ABC's coverage of the NATO bombing of Yugoslavia, and covered Pakistan after we lost the World Trade Center in 2001. He covered the Russian war in Afghanistan, Hurricane Katrina in New Orleans, the Asian tsunami, and the war in Iraq. In December, 2005, Bob became co-anchor of ABC's *World News Tonight*. A few weeks later he was seriously wounded in Iraq by an improvised explosive device (IED). During his thirteen-month recuperation, he and his wife, Lee, wrote a book called "In an Instant: A Family's Journey of Love and Healing".

With that as a suitably impressive introduction, Bob took the podium. He told the audience what a pleasure it was to return to

Cranbrook's campus, to be there that day with his parents in the audience. And he expressed how happy he was to see people from the old days, such as Arlyce Siebert, Charlie Shaw – "one of the best coaches and teachers ever," and Mickey Price, his history teacher – and skiing and soccer coach – who taught him, even while riding in chairlifts, that it was critical to learn history. He remembered the late Jake Jacobus, a teacher who gave him an appreciation of great literature and dogs – Jacobus had brought his dog to class. Bob said that while hairstyles had changed and prices risen since leaving Cranbrook, the school still served him as a teaching institution, and what he'd gained from it most recently was the opportunity to meet and know Miles Levin. He spoke about meeting Miles and Nancy at Detroit Metropolitan Airport, learning of Miles' grave medical condition, and discovering that they were to be co-speakers at the commencement ceremony for the Class of 2007. Then Bob said, "I've never really met a senior with more courage and guts than Miles. And he has told us what it means to live life without fear, but with joy. There are very few things you can predict in this life, but so far you have the best education in the world, and so much more to learn."

As examples of life's unpredictability, he told of his formal education and career in law and how, in covering the Tiananmen Square massacre, he came to understand that his life should be dedicated to journalism. Bob spoke of living in ten cities with his wife, Lee, while raising their four children. And of his brief, twenty-seven-day stint as a news anchor before suffering life-threatening injuries as the result of a roadside bomb while reporting from Iraq.

He addressed the students, telling them that they should expect study to be a constant in their lives. Never-ending change would require that they study life to keep up with it – that there would be so much more to figure out in business, race issues, global warming, faith, politics, and war. He said, "When you find the truth, speak it out … and don't forget to vote. You are this country's future."

As he was closing, he referred back to the yearbook he'd examined in preparing his speech. He said how odd it was that the inspirational quotes he had written in his yearbook addressed what he had gone through in life, and what Miles had gone through. In his yearbook he had written quotations from Henry David Thoreau and Adlai Stevenson that he still believed.

From Thoreau: I wish to live deliberately and not when I came to die discover that I had not lived.

And from Stevenson: So live decently, fearlessly, joyously, and don't forget in the long run it is not the years in your life but the life in your years that counts.

Then he looked at Miles in the audience, and included him in the company of Thoreau and Stevenson.

"Now today there is a new writer: the brave, young man who offers a real message on his website. The young man I love – your colleague, our friend, a teacher – is Miles. On his website, which I'm sure you've all read, is this quote which really struck me, because it is exactly what we know. 'If my struggle with cancer galvanizes actions of goodness, I can rest assured that, even if I succumb to the rogue cells, I will leave behind a legacy of victory. Dying is not what scares me; it's dying having had no impact. I know a lot of eyes are watching me suffer and – win or lose – this is my time for impact.'"

Woodruff paused and looked out across the gathering and continued.

"All those years ago, I sometimes wondered exactly what that 'Aim High' statue [of an archer] was, here at Cranbrook. What is that? But now I think I know that it is not about the hardness of the arrow or the strength of the bow; it is the place and the target you decide to shoot at ... whether a goal you know now or one you discover in the years ahead ... victory is in your ultimate impact. So aim high my friends. This is a special place on earth. Thank you, Miles. Thank you all, and good luck."

I had not expected Woodruff's speech to be so inclusive of Miles. That he gave so much of his seven minutes to Miles reflected Bob's incredible generosity, sincerity, and loyalty. Bob and Miles recognized one another as fellow warriors. This famous, forty-five-year-old journalist and this freshly-minted young man had each had – although in different theaters of war – the closest of brushes with death. They had formed a strong bond and were intensely devoted to one another. How totally wonderful and good it was that such a bond was among Miles' experiences in his brief life.

All of the students knew Miles' name and situation, but something big happened when Bob Woodruff trained such a bright spotlight on Miles. I believe a deeper impression was made that there was a genuine hero among them. During the awarding of the individual diplomas, which followed Bob's speech, the audience was asked to refrain from any applause until all diplomas had been given out. This restriction was occasionally violated by a solitary hooter or some clappers. But when Miles name was called, the entire class unhesitatingly erupted into a strident standing ovation. I caught a glimpse of Miles and his hand was covering his open mouth in an "Oh, my god" gesture. He was genuinely surprised by the energy which greeted the calling of his name. Then this pale, frail young man made his way to the podium where Arlyce Seibert and Charlie Shaw waited with open arms. The applause did not stop until he returned to his seat, his eyes glistening with tears. Mine were, too.

The graduation ceremony was followed by an al fresco luncheon held in a fountain court on campus. Miles was noticeably weak, but he pushed himself to participate.

When he finally got home, he composed an elegant note.

> There's silence now. We watched the train in the distance, chugging steadily closer and closer, until finally it was passing us by – first prom, then graduation earlier today. I've just come home and I'm at my computer now. I still have my tie on. My room is a travesty of quietude: there is stillness now, but the calm formed so abruptly that it feels paradoxically alarming. The last of the compartments have just gone whooshing past and the clanging has suddenly ceased. This weekend holds a slew of parties where we will be able to strain our ears and hear the sounds growing fainter in the distance.

What clarity of vision he had in that moment, what maturity!

CHAPTER SIXTEEN

KEEP FIGHTING

It is said that there are three tragedies in life. One is getting something you don't want. Like cancer. The second is not getting something that you do want. Like a future. The third is the tragedy of getting what you want. Miles was touched by all three of these. The goal of graduating with his classmates had served to propel him forward in life. Having achieved that, having struggled for it, he was feeling some emptiness now. The train had picked up his classmates to take them on to the next station, college – and would continue, without him, on its way to other stops – career, marriage, children, and other joys of life. But I wanted him to know that something of him would be carried forward by, and in, his classmates. And I wanted to emphasize to him that there was lasting value in what he had accomplished. So, on Father's Day, I posted a CarePage update that was an open letter to him.

June 17, 2007 The Father's Day Update

Dear Miles,

As many in this world now know, our ability to keep you is in question. Many now share the burden of carrying the weight of this sad prospect. And many participate in our continuous hopes, prayers, and efforts to banish the menace at our doorstep. But as much as they may want to help, there is a weight that cannot be removed from the mother or father facing the loss of a child. On this Fathers Day, I share some thoughts from the father's perspective.

Nina recently brought me a dozen school notebooks for recycling. As I was stacking them for transport to the bin I looked through one and saw that it contained hundreds of hours of carefully constructed notes, outlines, diagrams, definitions, proofs, etc.; all evidence of a superior education gifted to her by her maternal grandparents. In thinking about how she could so casually part with this considerable work of hers, I realized that their value was not in the having but in the making, in the doing, not the keeping. Therein I

123

find strength in dealing with the prospect of losing you. For when I look at what you have made and done, in the last two years alone, my pride becomes a salve to my pain. I recall discussing with you, before we knew of your illness, about life's Golden Moments. I said that a normal lifespan of some seventy years contains very few golden moments, maybe two or three at best. What are golden moments? They are those moments where chance and readiness intersect; Moments to which Bob Woodruff referred in describing some of his life's transitions. They are the brief moments Shakespeare refers to as that "tide in the affairs of men, which taken at the flood leads on to fortune; omitted, all the voyage of their life is bound in shallows and in miseries." Although it appears that chance has not been kind to you, chance nevertheless presented you with an opportunity which you took, prepared or not. If it turns out that your life has only one Golden Moment, it becomes ever more terribly important that you took it, that you grabbed it when it was yours to take. And that you did so gives me further peace about our dilemma. Thank you for that Father's Day gift.

Miles, in your high school graduation speech, you talked about the duties that come with privilege, the duty to put your good where it will do the most for others, the responsibility to make the most of your opportunities. You suggested that one could be a good janitor but that it might not be the optimal use of one's talents. I see this as a challenge I face each and every day. From the moment my soul is returned to me each morning I face the choice of indulging in laying abed a little while longer or getting up without delay and getting vigorously to the business we are all in - repairing the world. For myself, and I believe for many people your life has touched, your example gives us that kick in the butt we need to get right out of bed and get moving. And the threat to your life reminds us that we cannot defer our good works to a string of tomorrows. I truly believe that there will come moments in the lives of your classmates, for years to come, where they will derive inspiration and heightened courage from the example you have made of your life. Thank you for that father's day gift. A father wants to be surpassed by his son (or daughter) in education and accomplishment. You gave me that gift. You gave me gifts I was meant to give to you. You have travelled further up the roads of courage, grace, and acceptance than ever I have travelled. And you have taught me and stimulated me through example to be uncomplaining and unafraid; to face life and death with courage; to draw lessons and blessings from discord and conflict; to not just enjoy the richness of this earth, but to toil. And you have earned the privilege of exulting in the heights you have gained through a tough, grueling, arduous, exhausting, frightening, nearly ceaseless assault by a merciless foe. I pray that you may exult in such heights for many days to come, and that you may have life for many years to come. I am terribly sorry that your life is in jeopardy, your march has been long and hard, and I am deeply proud of you. Thank you for that Father's Day gift, love Dad.

I received some lovely messages in response to this. Pamela H. wrote "it's all clear now … wow … now I understand why Miles' words have exploded across the world … this latest post from the dad just melts my heart. Thanks to 'the Dad' for allowing us to share in your Father's Day."

Miles' readers also continued to express gratitude for his example. A woman from Iowa wrote the following.

"I've been following Miles pages for quite some time now and decided that I must let you know how Miles has touched my life. I am a single mother of 2, recently divorced and struggling with the path my life has taken. On many days, I am overcome with the loneliness and sadness that divorce has brought to my life. In following Miles' journey, I have realized that, even though life can be altered by circumstances, it is still life and it is ours to cherish. Miles has shown me strength. Miles, because of you, I hug my children a little tighter and a little longer. My little girls and I pray for you at night and are very thankful that God guided us to Miles' journey. Much love from me and my little ones and God Bless."

And thousands of others wrote at all hours of the day and night in the days surrounding his graduation:

"… when I saw your face on CNN I felt the hand of God."
"Unlike you, I'm kind of an unwilling survivor, surviving disabled from a car accident that killed my husband … Miles, you are an example to me."
"You have changed my life. Period."

"I am the mother of an 8 year old son who has been down the Rhabdo battle road. Michael gets so excited when they replay your segment (on CNN) and he says 'There's Miles!' You have inspired him. He says that he is going to be on the news when he graduates, just like you ... Please know that there is a little boy in New Jersey who thinks you are the real 'Superman'."

"The lives you have touched, the hearts you have lifted, the way you have taught me ..."

"...I felt terrified of death. Then, about a month ago I was introduced to your blog, and it has completely re-invented my outlook on life and death."

Perhaps it was seeing his continued impact that brought Miles, after a brief lapse, back to his readers, even though the news was grim:

June 23, 2007, I'm Back. For awhile now, with every significant event or experience that's come along on the strange journey I call my life, I've had to consider, "Am I going to share this on CarePages?" It's not an evaluation most make on any sort of frequent basis. For me, I do distinguish this from a diary. This is not my diary, but I believe candor (if appropriate) is courage, and I believe the world could use more of it. In light of this, I've decided to share something with you which I'd normally keep to myself: I was asked what college I was going to by a friend tonight. Now I can say I know what it's like to be harpooned in the chest. He is one of the most well-meaning people I know, so I know he didn't know too well what his words meant.....I had to tell him I'm not going to college in the fall. Though I didn't say it outright because it would almost feel explicit, it doesn't look like I'm going to college next fall either, or in any subsequent fall. Dr. Wexler has said point blank that, barring some scientifically unexplainable miracle, I will die from this disease.

I met a blind person tonight. To speak of him merely as "a blind person" is a disservice, because he defied his handicap in what is surely an effort requiring true valor. As was within his power, he did not let blindness keep him from seeing the world, and I aspire to be like him. I think my "success" with cancer would not have been possible (and I can't say those words without mentioning my mom, family, medical team, and friends) without being young. A world-weary person would be too brittle in their soul. But I watched this blind boy dance (with) total freedom at a concert and I couldn't help but try to appreciate how much harder he has to work at a life lived amongst company who get it for free and take it for granted. Yet I think it's fair to say that I can empathize in that regard. I talk with my friends about the fall and the future, and yes, I'm happy for them. And yes, my heart is pierced with envy.

A few days later, Miles posted an update of deep beauty, one that was poignant, sincere, and wise. It was also searing and soul-wrenching, and contained a phrase that quickly became his sound bite: Keep fighting; stop struggling.

I have some unfortunate news. It appears that my chemotherapy is no longer effective in containing the growth of my cancer. We knew this day would come from the moment I resumed chemotherapy treatment in March; the response for relapsed Stage IV rhabdomyosarcoma is ineludibly temporary. I'm flying to New York on July 5th for scans and most probably some form of investigational treatment (there are no other chemotherapy options left). We're buying one way tickets. My mom told me today that I don't need to go ahead with any more treatment if I don't want to. I want to. Mainly because life is the most breathtakingly amazing thing I could ever imagine. If I can get more of it, even just a couple more days or weeks or months, I'll fight pretty hard for that. It's not that I have a particularly high opinion of human or universal nature. While there is much good in the world, I see plenty of cruelty and abhorrence, but the stunning beauty and mystery of the experience in all its breadth and glory so profoundly surpasses words that I'm just going to shut up and move on to the next paragraph.

When Dr. Wexler told me I'd relapsed, so much hope collapsed in that instant that I asked him why bother resuming toxic chemotherapy simply to buy me more time. At my Cranbrook graduation, he looked me in the eye and said, "This is why bother." Dr. Wexler, this is the part where I admit that I was wrong and you were right.

I will fight to the bitter end. However, we must stop struggling. It is all but a certainty that I will never be cured of rhabdomyosarcoma. It is possible that I will die within weeks, and very probably within the coming months. Please don't tell me about someone you know who defied the odds; I'm aware people have. I hope to. But I'm not counting on it.

Keep fighting; stop struggling. Because as long as we are feeling at least physically and mentally decent, we will never want to leave. There will always be things we'll wish we could do or could have done differently. One day, written on the calendar in invisible ink, you will die. When that future date becomes today, I guarantee you'll wonder how the hell that happened. But once you accept it as part of the territory, it doesn't sting quite as bad.

I feel relatively ready. I'm proud of myself, proud of my life, and most proud of the story of my life. I say the story because it includes everybody in it and all the goodness that has transpired, the courage displayed by my family, the generosity of people like Bob Woodruff to have reached into my life—a busy and important man finding the time to call me from Syria during my chemo week. I am proud of the people my friends have become. They've grown so tall. I am most proud of myself (to answer the question) for my seeming ability to bring out the best in those around me wherever I may go. **What I've done, I believe, is what I've been sent here to do.**

Something has shifted inside me. Everything is okay now. It's okay because I am okay with it. The goodness that my having and dying from cancer creates in the lives of so many thousands of people overshadows and outweighs any personal bad. I'm in escalating pain from the tumors but I hardly mind. You know why?

This is my story and it's not meant to be told any other way.

All good things must end. When they do, sadness is unavoidable. This is one of the core reasons why Buddhists believe life is suffering. Take a romantic relationship, for example. While it can bring temporary happiness, the end is inevitable and so is the suffering. So monks are celibate. They're totally right too. Love hurts. But there's a "but," and it is this: it's worth it.

Whatever it is, it's going to end, and when it does, if you can say, "I enjoyed that," that's as much as you can be given (the sorrow comes standard), So let that be enough. Every rose has thorns.

The messages, from readers worldwide, became an internet brushfire of emotion and compassion.

One such message was: I read your most recent post while I was at work. It made me cry and I'm still crying …You came here and did what you were supposed to do. And, oh my God, you did it so very well!

Nancy decided to compose and post an update which gave some well deserved attention to Nina.

June 28, 2007 The Wind Beneath his Wings

Let me tell you a little bit about Nina, Miles' sister, soul mate, and best friend. This is like the situation in the Oscars when an actor or actress is nominated for Best Supporting Actor, but only because she is not well known and if she were, there's no doubt that she would be, and should be, nominated for Best Actor. And win.

Miles should have had a transfusion today, but delayed it by one day in order to have lunch with Nina, who leaves tomorrow (with ambivalence) for a month in France. I took Miles directly from the hospital to the Japanese restaurant (their favorite) to have a final meal together. And, the gripping part is that it just may be their final meal. I could barely find my car - through my tears- as I left them together, laughing and loving, just being near each other. One of my deepest pleasures in life has been their connection, which was apparent from day one. (I call them salt and pepper shakers: Miles is the salt, Nina is the pepper. They are like a little old couple who have been married for years, feeling completely comfortable with each other and companionship is enough.) My favorite photos from their childhood are those in which they are laughing together and she is looking at him with total adoration: her hero.

But, back to Nina. Her quiet struggle has been no less challenging, excruciating, and devastating - perhaps even more so. Her strength, her dedication, her admiration has been exemplary. Her feelings are not simple, and frequently they confuse even her. Yet, she holds on with fierce insistence to her love for Miles, which I hope she knows will never die. Make no mistake about it; she has been the wind beneath his wings.

I am frequently struck with the overwhelming awareness that, as hard as others try and want to, the pain of this experience is only really known and understood by others who themselves ache from this wound. Nina, too, is encountering the separation and it brings loneliness. Unfortunately, this is a pain that must be endured -

I say "must be" because we love Miles, totally and completely, and if there were no pain now, there would have been no love; they go hand in hand.

A few weeks ago, I announced that I pray for strength, not outcome. I include in that prayer some strength for Nina. It's not easy to lose - all in one -a best friend, an older brother, a laughing companion, and a hero. Through these last two years, Nina, too, has blossomed. Her sensitivity, her insight, her maturity "blow me away" and will serve her. This is a bookmark in her life, but it's not her book. She, too, will find her way, having been enriched by having loved and been loved from day one; that is a rare jewel, the facets of which are only beginning to shine.

The proud mom of two wonderful children

Having returned to Sloan-Kettering with Miles for scans and radiation, Nancy wrote from New York, on July 5, to say some things about Miles.

I started my tribute to Nina by saying, 'Let me tell you something about Nina'. Now, I say, as the mother who has known Miles since before he was Miles, 'Let me tell you something about Miles'; the quality about him that I think is most emblematic of his essence. Unlike almost anyone I know, Miles has no malice. He has not a mean bone in his body. That pool of purity is at his core and from it he radiates his wisdom, his kindness, his innocence, and his acceptance of all that is. He came that way. I always knew that Miles was not like most humans, but it was only when I identified this quality - the absence of malice - that my belief was confirmed. As I have watched the unfolding of his cancer journey as it has exploded into what could only be a divinely choreographed phenomenon, I see that it is that center in Miles, that universal love that is both the cause and the effect of the impact that he longs to create.

I have more to say on this (of course), but will leave you for now. Being the protective mother I am, you can rest assured knowing that I am surrounding Miles with love, care, and nourishment, and that I've erected a barrier between Miles and all forces evil. I am a sentinel. Miles will post when he is able. Miles' Mom.

CHAPTER SEVENTEEN

RECOGNITION

Miles did post on July 7, 2007, telling his readers that he had received good news – his vital organs were stable, and bad news – the cancer had entered his skeletal system and was causing bone pain.

Our plan of action is to first get the bones under control, then return to systemic treatment--maybe a different type of chemotherapy, maybe one of the newer biologically-targeted treatments. Sometime early next week I will receive an injection of a radioactive isotope designed to seek out cancer cells in the bones, delivering to them a dose of radiation. It's hard to tell how I feel about the news. Ambivalent, I suppose. The first part is better than I expected, the second part is worse. I wish the two would cancel each other out, creating basically what I expected, but unfortunately it doesn't work like that. We have to learn to respect surprise. Its power is not well appreciated, able to leave us dazed and reeling in the blink of an eye. But at least it doesn't look like we'll be surprised by any immediate serious complications. Certainty (relative) is golden.

Then, two days later, Miles had news that was all good.

The Sarcoma Foundation of America, an organization advocating for increased funding for sarcoma research and treatment programs, has named me the recipient of their 2008 Leadership in Courage Award which ... "is the highest award presented by the Sarcoma Foundation of America. It is given annually to a sarcoma patient who, through his or her public or private actions, writings or personal efforts, resulted in inspiration to other sarcoma patients that they do not have to be physically, emotionally or spiritually defeated by sarcoma or a diagnosis of sarcoma. Previous recipients have included U.S. Senator Mark Pryor, Edward Kennedy, Jr., actor Robert Urich, best-selling author Carole Radziwill, and renowned sarcoma patient rights advocate Rose Burt.

The Board of Directors of the SFA all feel Miles Levin's story of courage and inspiration in his battle with sarcoma makes him an eminently qualified person to receive this award."

They later said they were so pleased I decided to accept the award, which leads me to believe they understood the likelihood that I would decline due to my busy schedule, and my meetings with secret government higher-ups. As if. I laughed at their uncertainty because it is a truly flattering, humbling honor.

The schedule really is a bit tricky though as they present the award at their annual gala in New York...in June '08. As I probably won't be able to accept the award in person, we plan to videotape my acceptance speech and then show that at the gala. My family will be present. So big news of the good variety. I receive my radioactive isotope treatment today. The entire treatment is given in a single dose. It'll come just in time, too, as the pain (particularly in the tumors on my spine is escalating. And if you ever doubt my dedication to CarePages, I wrote this update with a 103.6 fever).

When his platelets were measured prior to the isotope administration, his levels were so low that it was decided the treatment could not be safely administered. Miles retreated from the hospital to the Ronald McDonald House. In the elevator he spoke with a girl wearing a chemotherapy pump on her back. She told him her temperature had reached 103. He humorously said that he had her beat by one degree. They laughed. The next day Miles fired up his laptop in a hospital waiting room.

Sometimes, during the good times, fun and laughter create themselves. But when things aren't so easy, you have to be the one to make it happen. It's quite possible, I assure you, but it takes work. It takes being able to lie in bed with that 104 degree fever, shivering uncontrollably, in pain, vomiting, and knowing that all your other friends are, at that very moment, partying or traveling or otherwise living up the summer and preparing for college—all of which are personal impossibilities—and still stay upbeat.

Yesterday was a good day. My pain was less than it has been. I had coffee with a Camp Simcha friend. I'm fighting to carve out an enjoyable experience in my remaining and compromised life, to the fullest extent possible, even in the face of escalating pain and diminishing functionality. Even though I'm pretty sick now, I refuse to surrender my zest for life. I'm writing this from the waiting room, in a wheelchair. I'm in a wheelchair, but I can be seen using it less as a crutch than as a high speed vehicle, zooming around the pediatrics floor getting coffee mochas and rolling on up to the computer stations, with such quick acceleration, sharp turns, and high cruising speeds that the ambulatory people drop their usual wheelchair pity gazes and jump out of the way in alarm.

I still have much to learn in the realm of making the best of it, but I like to think I know a thing or two by now. It is within your power; I know that much. It's hard; I know that too. But it's all in how you look at it. So have a little fun.

One thing that has helped me feel successful against my cancer is balance. Balance is different from level-headedness. It includes level-headedness, but it includes everything, including sometimes letting your emotions get the best of you. Whatever life brings, take it at face value. Let yourself experience it without judgment, at least initially. That comes after. Balance is fully accepting cancer on its own terms, as an unbounded experience, and then setting your own terms as to how you will continue to live your life.

The following Friday morning, June 13, 2007, Miles and Nancy took a cab from the Ronald McDonald House to the home of Nancy's brother and sister-in-law, Wayne and Nancy Alpern. Miles sat down on a couch with Matthew Alsante, Executive Director of the Sarcoma Foundation of America (SFA). A videographer was present to make a recording to be played at the SFA's awards gala. Matthew introduced Miles and, on behalf of the SFA, presented him with the crystal glass "Leadership in Courage Award".

Miles, just shy of nineteen-years-old, took the award into his hand, turned to the camera and without looking at notes or a teleprompter, spoke these words:

For so many of us, meaningfulness is a precious little gem buried somewhere at the bottom of our idle day-to-day tasks and worries. Yet certain things in the world sing to us a sublime wake up call. We're constantly searching for them – something real to hold onto and give us the feeling that our lives count for something worthwhile. Whatever this means to us personally, and we should not limit ourselves as to where we may expect to find significance or what form it may take – these special experiences, notions, relationships, and phenomena – they are what we experience as the profound. They mean something in very much the same way that Entertainment Tonight means nothing. And when we find it, we know because we can say, 'Now this ... this is life.'

Dealing with cancer is life. It is real life in full grit and glory. And, as I'm sure you already know, it forces to the forefront of our thoughts some very profound philosophical reconsiderations and, ultimately, resignations. We have to admit that the universe is more cruel and random than we would like it to be. To look into the eyes of a child with cancer is to look into the face of total injustice.

There are many things that are unfair in this world, such as poverty and political corruption, but childhood cancer touches a very special nerve, wrenching especially deep into our souls. It hurts us to see a child prematurely stripped of their innocence, forced at the age of eight to confront the possibility of dying. It hurts when I've had to lie alone in a hospital bed on a Friday night, knowing that, at that very moment, all my friends were out being young and wild and oblivious. It hurts to see the pain on the faces of the moms, dads, and siblings. It hurts me to see a bright future truncated when I know what they will be missing: the thrilling freedom of a new driver's license, the splendor of a first love. We mourn for what they will never have. Those older than I mourn for what I'll probably never have: the college experience, a profession, marriage, children, grandchildren, retirement. And believe me, I mourn too.

But I know that I've had something very special happen in my life, and it has nothing to do with any of that. Every day, I get countless emails from people around the world, telling me how profoundly I have changed their lives through my blog, that they look at the world through new eyes, that I have helped bring them peace in their own struggles. Maybe this is where my good does the most, even if that means I must die young. I do my best to embrace my sacrifice in happiness.

Life is not tragedy, but tragedy is life. When we come face to face with the tragic, we are more alive because of it. Our emotions of sadness and despair vivify the human experience, elevating it above the daily mundane. And by testing our love, hardship thereby strengthens it. Anything that builds character is inherently uncomfortable. And yet in the face of all the hopelessness that cancer brings, more dismal and morbid than can be found in almost any other corner of the world, I have witnessed hope such as I have never known. In the trenches of despair, I have seen unparalleled optimism and courage. In our struggle with cancer, it somehow finds a way to be a testament to all the good in the human character. I once wrote in my blog that it seems to take the darkest, bleakest of human tribulations to bring out the best in us and allow us to rally around what really matters. The families and friends in the ring with cancer, they display with a fullness rarely seen in ordinary circumstance, the almighty power of love. We know what sacrifice really means. It's long term, and it's unconditional, and it's found overwhelmingly in the world of cancer. You see, the families here, we are an army. We raise our swords against the very nature of the universe, against the short end of the stick, against the biological onslaught taking our soldiers from us every day. We are an army.

I have received abounding kindness from my nurses, almost to stick it to the cruelty of a situation we cannot control. And maybe to spite the random forces beyond our influence, I see doctors working themselves to the point of exhaustion, dedicated in the desperate pursuit to save another life from this relentless disease. I see courage in the parents who have given up their professions to become full- time caregivers. I see pure guts in the patients, taking it each day at a time, whatever the ride may bring. But most of all, as I step out of the elevators onto the pediatric oncology floor, I see love. I see it all around me. In a very deep way, cancer brings us together, binding us in a warm and understanding love. And for all the bad that cancer brings, this gift is priceless.

I'm not really sure I believe in all those biblical miracles like the splitting of the red sea, but I've talked with other families in waiting rooms and at The Ronald McDonald House and we've laughed about all sorts of things, including cancer. And I think to be able to find oneself at the center of hell and still find a way to smile at the flames – that's a miracle if I've ever seen one. So thank you from the bottom of my heart for this award. I can only hope to live up to the noble reputation of the good work being done here at the Sarcoma Foundation of America. You should all be so proud of yourselves for who you are and what you strive for.

Thank you.

CHAPTER EIGHTEEN

NEW YORK

Miles' "bucket list" – things to do before he died – was getting shorter. He had graduated from high school, had applied and been accepted to Kalamazoo College. He'd recorded his Sarcoma Foundation award acceptance speech. He had completed his chemotherapy, and visits to doctors and hospitals were getting fewer and shorter. He understood that he was about to enter a new stage, the stage of winding things up. Miles wondered if he could do so without the abandonment of hope.

Exactly thirty days prior to his death, he wrote about doing his best.

We've moved on to the next thing, the biologically-targeted treatments. Unfortunately, over the past several days, I've only gotten worse and worse. Dr. Wexler says it is too early to conclude definitively that the treatment is not working. We will give it the benefit of the doubt and continue the course for about another week, but we are all starting to get concerned now that it's not working, especially as there is no backup parachute after this, except hospice care.

My mom was saying that in some ways I am having this happen at the worst age, because it is usually such a time of hope—setting off to college with a future so full of possibility, a time of coming into your full potential. But then this comes along, and how could I possibly feel that way? How can I keep hope alive? It's so important to me, my faith in goodness. As I lay there in my hospital bed yesterday, my reality sunk in a little further, hitting in a new way—more visceral and immediate. The end seems to be rushing toward me now. This is my last bullet, and after one week of treatment, things are moving in the wrong direction. While I hope to God that next week brings a mysteriously delayed improvement, my back is against inevitable wall now. So if I can't find much hope in my own situation, I've decided I must look elsewhere. And that's when I remembered all that has transpired through my having cancer, of the profound change for the better in so many thousands of lives.

That always helps. An argument could be made that what has happened is for the greater good. I must hold fast to that, although it is hard at the moment.

I realize I'm looking for solace in altruism, but I don't know of anywhere else right now. People don't die overnight, and I'm rather terrified of the decline. It won't be fun. I know I've done everything I possibly could to try and survive, and that makes it both easier and harder at the same time: easier because I have no regrets, but a harder existential pill to swallow. It's hard to accept that your best is not good enough. I'm so sorry for the pain my dying will cause so many people, particularly my family. But I have to work with what I'm given, and maybe this is what I must do now. I've done my best to show how a person lives with cancer, maybe now my final purpose is to show how to die with cancer. It will be nothing short of one of the greatest challenges any of us will ever have to face.

I hope I will continue to be able to post. Somebody will.

Upon reading this I was moved to write to David Thomas, my great friend in Omaha. "Miles' experience," I wrote, "pulls us out of the game of hiding from the harsh and fierce aspects of existence, and places before us the terrible, fierce, dangerous, destructive, devouring world as well as the sweetness and beauty of life in its complete and true form. Miles found a way to look at all of it with high strength and tranquility and thereby reached a spiritual self-exceeding reserved for high souls."

David replied, "Past all the pain and unfairness, you must be very proud ... Miles has been such a gift to us all. His transcendence of all that has befallen him, his greatness, it is – you are right – the province of only the highest of souls. Only a very few can give what Miles is giving. And we would be lost without such gifts ... Our thoughts and prayers are with you and Miles and Nancy and Nina."

My friend's praise led me to try to convey to Miles my pride in his accomplishments. On July 20, 2007, I wrote an open letter to him as a CarePage update in which I cited numerous joyous memories of our lives together. I told him that when I sped up the tape of my memories of the last two years in my head, I saw the great and awesome flowering of a soul. I likened it to the time-lapse photography used in televised nature shows. I said it is only at that speed that we can apprehend the miracles all about us. Perhaps that was putting things a little too poetically. The simple truth was that death was closing in. Miles was still able to walk, but his remaining strength and vitality were diminishing.

While in New York for his last visit to Memorial [Sloan-Kettering] Hospital, he was invited to go on a visit upstate, with Dr. Wexler, to Camp Simcha. It was a goodbye tour and a chance for Miles to spend some private time with Dr. Wexler. He accepted the invitation and while he was gone, Nancy took over the CarePage to post a substantive update in which she began to consider how she could advance Miles' legacy.

As we are moving through this phase, we are discussing Miles' legacy. Any thoughts you have on this would be welcomed. To the degree that I am able, emotionally that is, I am motivated to do what I can to help any and all families avoid this nightmare. There is something so fundamentally wrong about this situation: childhood cancer without adequate treatments. While I don't have facts to support my view, nevertheless I cringe when I hear people ask for funds to support research efforts to cure breast and prostate cancer, while pediatric cancer goes underfunded. We frequently hear, our children are our future, yet there is a disparity between that and our behavior. It seems obvious that a society with its priorities in order would recognize that pediatric cancer deserves whatever it takes to save our children. What has to happen for that value to translate into efforts to protect our most vulnerable, the ones who carry the promise of a better tomorrow?

While she still had the stage before Miles' return from camp, Nancy wanted to say something about Dr. Wexler's talent and dedication.

July 25, 2007

I'm not going to say too many complimentary things about Dr. Wexler here for two reasons: I've said it enough (he should know by now how I/we feel), but also because he tends toward the modest and private side and I don't want to embarrass him. What I do want to say is that he, and every other pediatric oncologist that I have had

---

the honor to meet, are an exceptional group in their dedication, their tireless pursuit of anything that will give their patients even one more day, and their ability to continue in the face of such loss.

There's good news and bad news about how competent, thorough, and focused our doctor is ---every single day and for every single patient. The good news is that we have done everything possible, considered and used every treatment currently available for someone in Miles' condition, we've left no stone unturned. This was due in large part to the skills and downright brilliance that our doctor brings to the table. The bad news is the same: we've done everything and it wasn't enough.

Feeling limited by the state of the art is a tough pill for me to swallow. I had never been confronted with a problem that couldn't be solved by the intellect, creative solutions, and pure determination. Accepting this outcome does not come easily, yet, like gravity, reality always prevails. We are surrendering, slowly; Miles is too, but with deep sadness. As Miles said, this is so NOT what we want. As I've said, I pray for strength."

Miles returned from Camp Simcha and reported to his readers, entwining strands of travel reporting with strands of "travail" reporting in his update. Perhaps more than any he'd previously written, I believe this post contains all the traits characteristic of his best self – courage, resoluteness, honesty, appreciation, and acceptance.

July 26

I escaped the city (and, to an extent, the overbearing grimness of my situation) for two days. I made the 100 mile journey from NYC to camp in upstate New York with my hero Dr. Wexler. This man deserves his own dedicated update and a whole lot more, but right now I want to tell you about a gas station. Located just off the highway where the outer fringes of urban New York turn to forest, there's nothing special about this gas station, except for the fact that we stopped there. We were in the initial phase of our vacation, when all the fun that is to happen is still to happen, where returning home is a distant prospect. The immediate future is free from worry. The freedom of a getaway is at its peak.

Camp Simcha is for Jewish (mostly orthodox) boys with cancer. Yes, I know: a very specific niche of people. Simcha means celebration or joy in Hebrew, and they couldn't have picked a better name. Totally contrary to what one would expect from a group of cancer patients, it is a place of non-stop energy. If cancer had brains I imagine it would be quite discouraged to see the electric vitality bursting from its victims. But what I treasure most about Camp Simcha is that everyone there gets it, without even needing to say anything. They get it, tacitly, and that's not something most teenage cancer patients experience with their regular friends. I came back to the city on Tuesday. Gazing out the window (as I love to do on long car rides), I was hit in a strange way when I saw that same gas station there on the other side of the road. The time spanning since my stop there with Dr. Wexler just two days earlier collapsed under its own weight. With both events now in the past, they seemed not to be separated by any meaningful interval of time at all. I felt like I had been there an instant ago.

Time is doing funny things to me now. Without a working treatment, my time left on this Earth is probably around 2-5 weeks. The treatment seems to be keeping the cancer in check, though we really aren't too sure what it is doing. Still, I can't get my mind around the possible brevity of my remaining life. It often doesn't seem possible. It's just too huge and strange and unbelievable. There's pressure on every moment, even though I can't get off my couch for most of them.

If I am nearing the end, I am trying to relax into it, to accept what is to be. I know that things are happening as they are supposed to happen, if not by divine destiny then by the overpowering forces of nature. I know this because I know that we have given this fight our all. We have left no stone unturned. I have fought my very hardest.

Now it's up to the greater powers, whatever they may be. It seems a certainty that my path was not meant to be ordinary, but while everyone wants to feel special, I find myself alternating between feelings of gratitude for all that my life has been, with the feeling that it's not asking too much to wish for more--to trade it all for a normal, obscure teenage existence in which I craved greater impact.

I'm getting quite a lesson in not getting what I want. Turns out it is one of the hardest we'll ever have to learn. I'm not a child anymore; I can't get away with throwing a tantrum. This is hard, and there's no easy way around that.

CHAPTER NINETEEN

GRACE AND GRATITUDE

As for the readers, there was ample evidence of their personal investment and deepening concern. Both the volume and intimacy of the messages was increasing rapidly. We were getting new readers every day as people learned about Miles – from reading about him in newspapers, from speeches given at local fraternal organizations, like Rotary Clubs – even by word of mouth.

Some who'd only been readers at the site decided to post comments, such as Jason Davison of San Francisco, California.

"I have been following your carepage since the CNN story … what would I, a man twice your age, who has had and sometimes squandered many more opportunities than you will … get to have in yours … say that could mean anything to you … I need to let you know that you have touched my life and become a friend to me. Because of what you have endured with such style and grace … I will carry part of that around with me through my life … I will take your name and your story, your legacy, wherever I go in my life and share it with the people around me … I've been so impressed by your intelligence, your insight, your gentle and compassionate attitude and your deep love of family and friends … So I will just say thank you my friend. Godspeed to you on your journey … rest with the knowledge that you have made a difference in the lives of others and you will live on in the hearts of thousands of us."

As Miles continued to weaken, Nancy, Nina, and I supplied more of the CarePage updates. On July 27, 2007, Nina, sixteen years old, contributed a touching essay.

I'm sad for Miles because he will not experience a full and normal life; but I am also sad for myself because I know that my one and only sibling will not be able to share mine with me. We will not grow old together, living long and happy lives. We will not visit each other in college, or attend each other's weddings. Our children will not have cousins to play with in the summer, and we will not be there for each other when our parents die.

We won't get ready for bed together in the bathroom at night, and we won't make cinnamon rolls on Saturday mornings. We won't drive home from school together, listening to music and talking about our day. We'll never eat Mom's classic delicacy (macaroni with peas) off of the coveted purple and green plates, and we'll never make each other laugh again. I'll never tell Miles to turn down his music because the sound is bleeding through the wall, and he'll never again tell me to stop singing so loudly. He'll never share with me a favorite quote from a quirky movie, and I'll never show him a new song that I've discovered. Never again will I yell at Miles without eliciting an equally infuriated response, and never again will I hear him crack his knuckles and ask me if his cologne is strong enough.

These things will only be memories now. And even though Miles would have been away at college this year and these familiar rituals would not have been practiced any longer anyways, it's different. He will be more than a phone call away, and I will have to recall the fondness of our childhood alone. There is no other person in the world besides Miles who understands the childhood euphoria that we shared.

The part of my heart that loves Miles has and always will be filled with the kind of deep and true love that most never have the privilege to understand for themselves. I will never miss him in my heart, because I know that he is always there. But it is in the tiny, mundane moments that slip through our fingers where I will feel his absence the strongest. The next time you find yourself all together as a family, cherish the moment.

Miles was steadily losing strength and his readers sensed it. Our doorbell rang every day with deliveries of flowers and gifts of every sort. The mail brought dozens and dozens of cards. Nancy thought about this outpouring of concern and generosity, composing the following updates on July 31 and Aug 1.

… At our house, we talk frequently about why this - the Miles phenomenon - has happened. Apart from destiny, why is it that Miles and his story and his way have touched so many hearts? Forget the reasons for a moment; what is clear is that Miles has created a spiritual community in cyberspace. From a sociological perspective, the complexity of the world we live in leaves us longing for community, which is now satisfied (in part) by the internet. The

CarePage community fulfills our need to belong - to some group. But it's more than that; it's the combination of Miles' uncanny writing ability, his compelling story of man against all odds, and his willingness to bare his beautiful soul so openly and honestly to anyone willing to sign on to his CarePage that has made him a hero, a source of inspiration, and a soul to love unconditionally.

I'm not sure that those reasons really or completely answer the question: why did this happen? Why, since Miles relapsed, has he received the public recognition, the adoration, and the encouragement that his fight has engendered? And in doing so, it has provided the necessary visibility of the horrors of pediatric cancer, which, as Miles said in his acceptance speech to The Sarcoma Foundation when he received The Award in Leadership and Courage (soon to be available to you) touches a special nerve. And now, for me, struggling to accept that I must go on without my companion in this fight, what does all this mean? ...

... In my reflections about the Miles' phenomenon, I realize that Miles grabbed the brass ring; he allowed himself to be transformed. The boy Miles was in June of '05 was sweet, innocent, disorganized and ungrounded ("earth to Miles"). The man that Miles is today is clear, focused, heart centered, and purposeful. It was cancer that intervened. That deadly disease carried the power of transmutation, and Miles accepted the offer. That's my answer to 'What is Miles' legacy?' - He turned something lethal into something life affirming. He is an alchemist.

On August 3, 2007, Miles wrote the first of his final two CarePage updates. This one was for his family.

August 03

This update has been a long time coming. I guess I haven't written it sooner because I'm afraid that anything I might say could never be adequate comeuppance for the gifts they have given me. I'm talking about my family, of their ongoing and abounding love, dedication, support, and sacrifice. I know I'll never be happy with this update. There is no way to say thank you for a gift so huge, but to not try would be worse.

It's a stupid system, but the only way to fully understand what you have is by losing it. Therefore, luckily for me, I'll probably never know how blessed I am to be enveloped in the sort of love my family provides, especially now. I can only try to imagine how much scarier this would be without them. I think it is safe to say without exaggeration that my mom has been the best mother I've ever met in person. All along she knew what she was doing. That is a rare confession from a teenager, but I cannot deny her talent and wisdom. She has a keen sense of how much to sculpt and how much to let take form on its own. She knows how to make her children feel loved. Of course, what has really revealed her exceptionality has been the tenacity of her love and efforts during these past two years. She stepped up to the plate and never backed down, learning about the disease, finding treatment after treatment, consulting with expert after expert. I am so proud and grateful to her. If it were not for Nancy Levin, I would probably have died months ago. In a period typical of parent-pubescent shouting matches, my mom and I have formed a rare sort of bond. We've become friends who understand each other on a deep level. I owe her so much credit for who I am.

As for my sister, she is truly my best friend. Nina and I don't fight. It is almost unnatural. In the rare instances that we do fight, we feel bad and work it out. What sort of mutant siblings behave in this manner I do not know, but I'm grateful for it. Maybe there's something about the fact that we're stuck together, that while friends come and go, she'll always be my sister. We would both go to the ends of the earth for each other.

And my dad. As I think of him, it occurs to me how unique he is. I've never encountered anyone else like him. He showed me how to be my own person. We share some very special memories: scuba diving off the coast of Venezuela, bicycling, skiing in British Columbia...the list goes on. I treasure these memories. It's been a privilege to be my father's son and we managed to have a great time along the way.

My family is not as strong as we present on CarePages. This is an incredibly hard time for all of us and we're each of us only human. But we are strong, we love each other, and we'll make it through.

Although Miles was physically weak and staying in bed most of the time, he was still managing his affairs. An issue came up related to some disappointment with a particular friendship. Clearly, a person knowingly in his last days is prone to be very discriminating with his expenditures of time and energy. Yet Miles found time to consider how to handle this particular disappointment. Nancy wrote of it in an update.

August 06, 2007

...MORE EVIDENCE THAT MILES IS NOT LIKE A NORMAL HUMAN

It might be tempting to think that a person as kind, sweet, and wise as Miles is would be a wuss. When I commented in an earlier update that he has no malice, without an expanded understanding of what that means, one might think that Miles is soft, mushy, and spineless, a pushover. Isn't that the definition of a wuss?

As recently as this past Saturday morning, when Miles has been feeling weak at best and sick and in pain at worst, he had the wherewithal to confront a situation with determination and clarity. He continues to amaze me with his integrity, his clearly defined set of values, principles and priorities, and most important of all, his willingness to act on them. He wrestles with decisions, evaluating often conflicting values, striving to identify the right course of action for him. He seems to be unafraid of recourse. He does not place a high value on popular opinion. He has the courage to face fallout. He is constantly guided by what he perceives to be a higher truth. Many times, when I've seen him trying to make a decision, I see that he looks for "the right thing to do", which frequently is the simplest, kindest, and most obvious.

To see this in Miles, at age 18 (nearly 19), while feeling so unvital, evokes my highest admiration for him. Watching him the other day consider many aspects of the situation before him, factoring in the circumstances, and then turning inward until an authentic decision emerged, placing integrity above all else, even his failing body...that is not a wuss.

Miles wrote his last update to his CarePage readers.

147

August 07, 2007

I'll warn you in advance: this isn't going to be much of a crowd-pleaser.

There is a shred of good news, I suppose, so we can start with that. I've felt worse in previous days than I feel today. I tried the experimental treatment sunitinib for a total of about three weeks. I've only gotten worse. Significantly worse. Some of my discomfort, we suspected, was probably being caused by the treatment itself. So we decided to take a couple days break from the treatment and see how that made me feel. Lo and behold, when discontinued, I felt a little better. The nausea was much less. Of course, discontinuing the treatment means my improvement will only be temporary before the cancer takes over. We have started an herbal extracts regimen. Nothing to lose at this point. Only to gain. I'm not resuming the sunitinib. It is pretty certain that all that continuing treatment would accomplish at this point is compromising the quality of my remaining time. We've set up hospice care to manage my decline from home in Detroit, which is where I am now and where I want to be. I'm not really having any visitors; this is a time for family. I'll try to update as I can, but I am getting worse pretty quickly.

I wish I could offer better news. I really do. All I can think to say is thank you. Thank you for your ongoing support of me and my family through this most difficult time.

CHAPTER TWENTY

LIFTOFF

After Miles' farewell to his CarePage readers, he became so weak that he couldn't handle the stairway alone. His last visitor, who was not a relation, was Robyn. She came in the early afternoon on August 8, and went up to his room where they cuddled in his bed. We left them alone and can only imagine the tenderness of their exchange. Robyn stayed for a couple of hours before quietly leaving. That evening there was a big, bright moonrise. Nancy, Nina and I helped Miles come downstairs. We sat on the front porch for about ten minutes looking at the radiant moon.

The next day, August 9, 2007, we had what we called our "final" conversations with Miles. Nancy went first, alone, and later wrote an update.

Have received word that the spaceship is on its way. Miles is packed and ready to go. He is taking nothing with him, except himSELF. He told me this morning that this process requires extraordinary patience.

He and I have had our final conversations, which were simple: LOVE. In our case, he and I acknowledge that there is nothing much to forgive. The "I'm sorry" part of the conversation was a nano-second. The gaze, which is what we do now most of the time, touches eternity. The bond between us is sealed. Our commitment has been solid, through thick and thin, until the very end. I rest easy in knowing that my devotion was 100%, at all costs, because my love was defined by sacrifice. I'm at peace with the feeling of completion, no regret, and no lingering self doubt. I was and am his mother – in every sense – until the end.

He is resting in the knowledge that he has accomplished his mission. Early on in his CarePages, he said something to the effect, It's not dying I'm afraid of; it's dying without having had an impact. I repeat: he is resting in the knowledge that he has fulfilled his purpose - in spades. Little does he know, really, how true it is and will continue to be so.

> The house is quiet, very still. No visitors; just family. This is how he wants it. The mood and atmosphere is heavy with waiting. I'm trying not to rush anything; everything in its own time. No more fighting or struggling. I pray he drifts away in peace. He deserves that.

After giving him some time, I went in for my "final" conversation. I sat down beside his bed and held his warm hand for a minute. We looked at each other and he said, "Dad, what about your job?" By "job", he meant my career which, by and large, had not exceeded the middle management ranks. I knew this was one of his concerns. I told him, truthfully, that although I hadn't been a good fit in the corporate ranks, I'd been very careful in saving and rather successful in investing and there was no need for concern. He said he hoped I would find a satisfactory outlet for my talents because they shouldn't go to waste.

Then I told him that I'd written something to say to him and asked if he thought he could hear it now. He nodded "yes."

"Dear Miles,

Our birthdays mark the completion of a year of life. You are close to marking the completion of your nineteenth year and the beginning of your twentieth. For most of your life it's been easy rowing. You were born into a rich country and into a wealthy, educated, principled family. You lived in a wholesome, supportive community. But in the last two years it's been very tough rowing. Your life of ease on calm waters very abruptly turned into a powerful storm; and you had to row against an adverse current and strong opposing wind. A life of bests became a life of tests. And so you set yourself to rowing. You applied your vital powers, but the storm would not abate. The things that sustained you, I believe, were a raw desire to live, a keen hope that this storm would pass, the love of your family, and the support of your community of friends. Your valiant efforts were witnessed by many, and your lack of complaint was noticed, and it made a great impression, and evoked pride and admiration, and rightly so.

It should be obvious you've made me a very proud father and you've elevated the family name, and you've elevated your own soul.

Miles, as you know, my life has not been lived along such clear lines of intensity and accomplishment, or of elevating the family name. But I assure you that my own rowing of my boat, for however long I have left, will be intensified by your example. You have my love, pride, admiration, and gratitude forever. I love you, Miles."

He patted his heart with his hands, looked at me and whispered, "Mission accomplished." After a minute of letting tears run down my face, I dried my eyes, kissed him on the forehead and left his room.

Nina had her turn with Miles as well.

The next day, August 10, Miles had enough energy to respond to a few questions from Nancy, which she posted as "a final interview."

August 10, 2007 A final Interview with Miles

As Miles is winding down his physical presence, I asked him to grant me one final interview. He agreed, provided it was brief. Feeling excited to again experience his grace; I took it, with that condition.

Q: Miles, many people have asked, what exactly your message is. Could you state it succinctly?
A: People like to construe that every day is a blessing, and that's not true. There's nothing wrong with having a bad day; they do happen. But (what's important is) that there's enough good out there- even if you have cancer or something terrible happens to you -you can still find it.
Q. Can you tell us what the "it" is?
A. The goodness and worthwhileness of enduring the bad day…because the world has so much to offer.
Q. What have you learned about life?
A. That it's unpredictable.
Q. What one thing stands out for you as something you are grateful for?
A. The relationships I have had with people – above all else. That's what endures.
Q. What do you want people to think about you when they think of Miles Levin?

A. Someone who maintained their light through their darkest journey.

Q. What qualities in humans do you value the most?

A. Kindness. I think it's one of the only things that helps everyone.

Q. Anything else about that?

A. If there is one thing that would make the world a better place, it's more kindness to all.

Q. Miles, what does "kindness" look like?

A. A general love for other people.

Q. Can you say how that translates into action?

A. Not really. (laughter) Who is to say I'm right about any of this?

Q. What advice would you give to parents on how to love their children?

A. Tell parents they are not their children. They are raising new individuals who are going to be different from them.

Q. So, how should parents influence their children?

A. It's a hard balance between controlling and permissiveness, and I don't know the answer. If I had to say, I'd say, ask my mom, she accomplished it.

Q. Is there anything you want to say about what's happening to you right now?

A. No, it's private, and I haven't worked through it yet.

Q. Anything else about anything?

A. I'm pretty much feeling done sharing. I would if I had the energy.

On Saturday, August 11, the four of us watched the Italian movie, "Life is Beautiful." Everything was calm inside and outside the house. I posted an update – which Miles never saw – a reflection on seeing him at rest.

August 12

… Miles, as I look at you abed this moment, the name for you that comes to mind is Prince Valiant. I don't mean prince as sovereign or ruler, but as one who is pre-eminent in his class. In addition to the affirmation of your teachers and classmates at Cranbrook, cancer patients and families from around the world see you as a prince of their realm. They trust and admire you as one who knows how to reflect their situation and their needs fairly and vigorously. You are a prince to them. And as for valiant, I swear I have never seen any human behave more stoutly, courageously, and heroically in facing an overpowering, pernicious horror.

But I have also had the privilege of seeing you lay down your weapons after a day of battle, and I have seen the soft belly of your own wants and needs. And the most terrible thing for me to bear has been to witness the gradual and understandable erosion of your keen, desperate hope that you might be spared the outcome this disease seems to want. I believe you take solace in knowing that you have inspired many to stand their ground and fight with more determination to tame this menace. Love, Dad.

Sunday evening was the Perseid meteor shower.

On Tuesday, Nancy posted an update letting readers know that we were taking it hour by hour.

Tuesday, August 14, 2007 MOM here...

I know August. I know the heat and slant of the sun, the sounds of birds at this time of the year, the smells of the days that are bridging summer and fall, the anticipation in the air as vacation winds down and school revs up. I know August, having lived it myself for many years, but I especially got to know August when I lived and breathed the unique qualities of August in 1988, when I was waiting for Miles to arrive; now I am waiting for Miles to leave. Anniversary reaction - in reverse.

Miles is dying in the same graceful, courageous, and honest way he has confronted every step of his illness. The hospice nurse told me that she has never seen a patient, of any age, with such openness and curiosity about the process, and she has been touched. He still looks beautiful, with his sculpted features, his long beautiful fingers, and his peaceful countenance. There is less and less of Miles, and more and more of just pure love.

Some days are "better" than others; some hours are "better" than others ----in terms of his comfort level, in terms of which world he is in, and in terms of his anguish and restlessness. He has made it clear: he wants out of this body. He's done.

We have created a bubble for the last ten days - peaceful, quiet, unthreatening, and preparatory. He can rest, uninterrupted, which he needs to do. Dying is demanding and exhausting.

153

Yesterday, some comfort was delivered - by Miles' Waldorf kindergarten teacher, she an angel. She sent many things, including some photos of him (and our family) at his school birthday party, age 6, a beautiful book about angels coming to earth which clearly was about Miles, a touching letter written in her beautiful, ethereal voice, and a piece of blue silk that she used when children needed love. Miles wrapped the silk around his head and shoulders and listened intently while I read the book to him, as I have done so many times before. Mrs. Long knew Miles' soul then, and now. Her card said, "I knew a boy who liked to dig."

Lee Woodruff sent me an email recalling our first meeting with her at the Detroit airport. "I believe that every so often someone who is angel-like is put on this earth to teach us something...they have qualities that most of us only aspire to - keen wisdom, superhuman strength, compassion and endurance, generosity in all of its forms, and the singular white heat of pure love. Miles is such a person. And we are all lucky to have known him for too brief a time."

Five days before he passed away, Miles received a letter from Dave Gross, a paramedic in Tiffin, Ohio. He'd previously sent Miles gifts of clothing with the Tiffin, Ohio paramedic squad's insignia. Dave wrote, "It is tough to talk to people that are dying, especially at such a young age. I experienced death many times in my paramedic career and it never gets easy … I wish I knew the right words to say to you and your family. I never read all your posts (but) I especially liked your comparison to life with hitting golf balls … You said the last balls in the bucket seem the most important that we hit them perfectly. I believe you really hit some awesome shots with your last golf balls. You have made more of an impact in your short life than most people make in 90 years. I truly hope your last days are peaceful and pleasant."

With everything so quiet in the house, and hardly any distractions or interference, Nancy took time to reflect on the level of exhaustion she felt. She wrote an update on behalf of mothers in caring for sick children.

Wednesday, August 15

The mom here ... to some extent, this applies to all mothers of children with cancer ... YOU HAVE NO IDEA ...

You have no idea how fatigued I am, way down to the bone. I don't think there's a word in our vocabulary that fully captures or conveys my level of exhaustion. Day in and day out, night in and night out, worrying, doing, balancing, pretending, carrying concern in every cell of my body, anticipating, arranging, considering, planning, advocating, protecting, hoping, wondering, AKA loving.

You have no idea how far behind I am with so many realms of life. The piles are moved from here to there, periodically thinned but never handled. There are items at repair shops that have never been picked up and probably have gone out of business. The items that need to go to a repair shop fill my garage, including my body. Life at my house is constant triage: regular review of exactly what has to be done i.e. can be deferred no longer. The endless "to-do" list has not included LEISURE for 26 months. Leisure is a concept that is as foreign as cancer was before June of 2005.

You have no idea how much of my life has been sacrificed in the service of fighting this tireless monster. I have given up my career; I have given up my social life; I have given up physical fitness; Fun has been so given up, it doesn't even qualify as something on the list of things that have been given up; I have given up my health; I have given up any hobbies; I have given up any illusions of peace and security. I have given up the idea that just because I'm a nice and kind person, the worst thing that could happen to a mother won't happen to me.

You have no idea how difficult it is to explain to others who are not in this boat what happens to your life. That's because, unless it's happened to you, you have no idea how consuming cancer treatment can be and is, especially in a family. The way you can tell that others don't understand is when, out of the goodness of their hearts, they suggest getting a massage or a manicure.

Soon, I'll have time for a massage AND a manicure, but no desire. Soon, my life can be mistaken for the Grand Canyon. Soon, I'll wonder where my life is and what I've been doing every single day for 26 months. I'll have to re-invent myself. One thing I know: it will look very different from the self I was before June 4, 2005.

> Despite all of that, I wouldn't have done one thing differently. And that's still true despite the ending of the story.
>
> P.S. One final YOU HAVE NO IDEA....
> You have no idea how many tears I've cried.

For days Miles had been in his bedroom unable to consume anything other than liquids and pain relievers, spending most of the time with his eyes closed. But on Friday, August 17, Nancy wrote this update.

> We received a gift this morning: a good half hour of a lucid and loving Miles. If I thought, or you thought, Miles displayed grace, courage and dignity before - during his two year ordeal - that was nothing. I now see the depth of this as I walk, right along side of him, through the demise of his physical body. I took advantage of these few moments this morning and told him this, how touched I am to see him maintain his humor, his manners, and his outlook even at the verge of death. His response: "glad I could help."

I found some old video cassettes in the basement. The labels indicated they were recordings I'd made when Miles was a youngster in Omaha, before Nina was born. A neighbor brought over equipment needed to play 8 mm tapes. We hooked it up to the television in the master bedroom and asked Miles if he'd like to watch the tapes. He said he would. I suggested using the wheelchair we had from hospice to move him from his bedroom. But he said that he could walk, so I advised using the wheelchair's handles to steady himself. With considerable effort he brought himself to a standing position and began pushing the empty wheelchair. Nancy and I walked beside him. He walked about fifteen feet, then collapsed before we could be of any assistance. The effort to stand and walk had consumed his meager stores of energy. With Nina's help, we lifted him onto the bed in the master bedroom. After letting him rest awhile, we played the cassettes. One showed him in 1989, at around age one, just laughing his ass off as Nancy made goofy gestures. He was literally a bundle of joy, reveling in the fact of his existence. But the Miles of 2007 was so depleted that he could barely open one eye to watch. His presence in this world was wavering. I was a few days too late with the videos.

I've decided that this book need not tell of every remaining moment of Miles' life. As I said at the beginning, the value of this book lies in Miles' comportment and his choices while facing death, not in his dying. After playing the videos from his childhood for him, we let him remain in our bedroom. I slept on the floor next to the bed. I awoke at around 2:00 a.m. and checked on him. He was breathing slowly and his fingers were slightly cool. I fell back to sleep for a few hours and, at around 5:00 a.m., woke again. Miles had quietly dropped his body sometime between when I'd last checked on him and held his hand, and 5:00 a.m. on Sunday, August 19, 2007. His shift was over. I woke Nancy to let her know that he had departed. We hugged and sat quietly, not seeing any reason to rush things. In Judaism, it's important that the body not be left alone from the time of death until burial. This is partly based on the belief that the soul is in transition, hovering in the vicinity of the body, and is comforted by the nearness of loved ones. Accordingly, either Nancy or Nina or I stayed with Miles for a few hours before deciding it was time to call the funeral home and let them do what they do. In the meantime, Nancy released an update.

Sunday, August 19, 2007

Miles' earthly body has left us....early this morning. This is the day we've been dreading since June of '05, fearing it would come, and now it's here. We did everything humanly possible to arrest this disease. Our efforts were not enough. There are no interventions currently available that could have produced a different outcome.

Talk about destiny, G-d's plan, purpose, anything you want, but the fact is that our boy, our beloved son and brother, was snatched from us, and it hurts. We knew it was coming, yet we are shocked. We knew it was coming, yet we were unprepared. We knew it was coming, yet it feels unreal. We knew it was coming, but we hate it.

Sunday morning. Miles should be having pancakes with Nina right about now. Instead, the three of us are wandering around wondering what to do with ourselves. Pacing has become my specialty. We do have some plans in place: a very small, immediate family only funeral; a big memorial/celebration down the road to commemorate Miles; and a lot of crying.

We ask that if you feel an inclination to send food or flowers that you transfer that impulse to our new fund (see below); it would be more satisfying to us to know that honoring Miles means helping another family.

At the moment, there is little consolation for the serious war we fought when in the end, we lost our warrior. We aren't ready to look at the legacy, the divinity, the gift. We're grieving the loss of our child and brother. The best advice I can offer anyone wanting to provide comfort is this view: this stinks, plain and simple. Please don't forget: Miles didn't just die; CANCER killed him.

Nancy, Jon,and Nina

UJF-Miles Alpern Levin Fund
P.O.Box2030
Bloomfield Hills, MI 48303
Attn: Susie Feldman
Telephone: 248-203-1461
e-mail: sfeldman@jfmd.org

By coincidence, I come to the end of writing this tribute to my son on a significant day in the Jewish calendar. Sunset tonight brings the first eve of Passover, when Jews all over the world gather together to retell their exodus story. A great portion of the Book of Exodus is devoted to precise instructions about how to prepare a resting place for God's presence – the tabernacle (Mishkan) – including the Ark of the Covenant, tables, an oil lamp, lace hangings, coverings, vestments for the high priests. In other words, a lot of cargo. Having spent four-hundred and thirty years in Egyptian bondage, Jews were not experienced as nomads. Had they understood the importance of their possessions being lightweight and portable, they might have shown more resistance to constructing something that used four tons of silver, one ton of gold and even greater amounts of Acacia wood, animal hides and stones. What they did understand was that they were making a sanctuary so that the one God might dwell among them. Once they had finished its construction, they undertook the formidable task of taking their sanctuary with them throughout their travels. Rabbi M. M. Schneerson wrote that they did so because they knew they were on a "journey that leads to the world to come. At every stop, we do all this place demands of us. At each encampment, we build our tabernacle anew – even if just for the moment. For each moment is an entire world, as precious as eternity."

Miles undertook his journey with equal vigor and commitment. He possessed the understanding that the way a person approaches a task influences how he will perform it. He decided that his part was to do everything demanded of him in the hope that he might have a full measure of this world. When it became clear that he would have less than a full measure, the short end of the stick, he determined to move through and on with grace and gratitude.

As his CarePage reader, Dirk Baezner, put it:

He accepted cancer without malice;
Inspired the world with Gentle Grace;
Welcomed heaven with open arms;
And left the world a better place.

During two challenging, compromised years, Miles Levin became an inspirational public figure; converted a confrontation with death into an opportunity for personal growth; produced numerous works of art in clay, paint, glass, and metal; and helped others be their best selves.

After his death:

- The Sarcoma Foundation of America gave him its Leadership in Courage Award.

- The Nature Conservancy named a tract of land in Michigan's Upper Peninsula in his honor.

- The Cranbrook Kingswood Educational Community established an annual student award in his name which is given to a student showing the greatest development of character and courage.

- The Mannes Institute for Advanced Studies in Music, New York, NY established the Miles Levin Essay Award.

- Dr. Richard Keidan, a Michigan-based cancer surgeon, established the Miles Levin Nepal Foundation for Health and Education to improve public health and sanitation in a number of remote Nepalese villages.

- The Miles Levin fund at the United Jewish Federation of Metropolitan Detroit was established to support families confronting pediatric cancer. Within its first weeks it received over $50,000 in donations, primarily in small contributions from hundreds of CarePage readers who knew Miles only through his writing.

EPILOGUE

Miles had said that life's value is in its impact; that we are the ripples not the stone. Because this book has been about his life, I want to segregate things about his death in this epilogue. In my opinion, his life and death elicited some written tributes that were of the highest order of which English is capable. I would not want to have closed the book without making a record of some of those tributes.

The Funeral

In late morning of Sunday, August 19, 2007, after the undertakers had come and gone, we called our immediate family to let them know that Miles had dropped his body and that we were going to have the burial the following day. There would be no chapel service, only a small graveside service under the guidance of Rabbi Arnie Sleutelberg, who had shepherded Miles through his Bar Mitzvah. The service was limited to Miles sister, parents, grandparents, aunts, uncles, cousins, and their spouses – altogether only eighteen people, scattered all over the country. In addition to the rabbi, we invited one person not related to us by blood: Charlie Shaw, head of Cranbrook's upper school. Charlie had agreed to offer a eulogy. We also readily assented to a request by Nancy's brother, Wayne, to offer a eulogy. We asked the funeral home to post an announcement on their website that the interment was private, with no visitation following. This was all by design. Nancy and I had predicted that following Miles interment we would want privacy and quietness, not the noise and distraction of hundreds of visitors. To give the few invitees time to arrive, we asked for the burial to take place as late in the day as the cemetery would allow, which was 3:00pm.

Monday was a warm and cloudy day, with rain predicted. At the funeral home an attendant (a shomer) had stayed beside Miles throughout the night, reading psalms in Hebrew. In the morning the attendant gave custody of the body to a holy society of volunteers (Chevra Kadisha) who bathed Miles body as part of a 2,000 year old purification ritual (Tahara) and dressed him in a white shroud (Takhrikhin). They placed his personal prayer shawl around him (Tallit) after removing a fringe to indicate that he was no longer bound by earthly obligations, and they laid him in an unvarnished, unlined coffin.

I had arranged to accompany the coffin from the funeral home to the cemetery. Nancy thought I should do so without her. So at around 1:00pm I set off in my car for the funeral home, twenty minutes away. There, I was met by a gentleman named Otto. Otto took me to a private room where Miles body lay in the coffin. The orthodox coffin does not try to seal off the body from the elements. It encourages re-assimilation into the earth by leaving the wood unvarnished and by drilling holes in the bottom of the coffin. It is also the orthodox custom to forgo viewing the body, in order to preserve the dignity of the deceased. But an exception is made for immediate family, and Otto had left the coffin open. He had done so because he wanted to offer me an opportunity to place small stones over Miles' eyes and mouth, a practice with which I had no familiarity. Otto left me alone. I stood at the open casket taking one last look at my beautiful son. I then placed the small stones over his eyes and mouth and closed the casket. There was a knot in my throat. I grabbed some tissue and sat down to quietly shed some tears. After a few minutes I ripped my shirt as a sign of grief and walked out of the room to let Otto know I was ready to go.

The two of us rolled the coffin to the hearse and into it through the rear hatch. He and I took the driver and passenger positions in the hearse and began driving to the cemetery, about eight miles away. It was raining just enough to require the intermittent wipers, a gentle weeping. We made a little small talk, but were mostly quiet. I found some satisfaction in knowing that this funeral was being carried out according to our wishes; and that it was so intimate and "hands on". I wished our arrival at the cemetery would have taken longer, but in less than twenty minutes we were at the cemetery's wrought iron entry gate. When we pulled in we could see that two limousines had delivered our family to a canvas canopy erected over an open grave. The rain had increased noticeably and, after parking near the limousines, Otto retrieved umbrellas for each of us. We opened the rear of the hearse and pulled the coffin half way out. We assembled six cousins and uncles as pallbearers to carry the coffin from the hearse to the lowering device positioned over the grave. Rabbi Arnie then conducted a service in which he recited a portion of a prayer called "Tzidduk Hadin" in which we accept God's judgment and he recited the "El Molai rahamim" which asks God to shelter the souls of the departed and bind their souls among the living that they may rest in peace.

Charlie Shaw's Eulogy

Charlie Shaw then stepped up to the podium and said:

"Today we form one body of utter sadness and woe. As one voice from outside the family, I have the strength to stand at their side for a moment to speak for the community of Cranbrook where Miles attained the measure of a man and leader. He blessed this school. He gave strength of purpose to our adults who have grown tired; he gave meaning to our lives, as today he gives us new meaning and purpose.

As Nancy observed, all great teachers keep their titles out of view. We saw Miles as wary about emotions such as consolation and sympathy, which can so easily elicit passivity and compliance. Instead the active force of kindness was what he asked us to embrace. Miles consistently seemed to suggest that the experience of guilt was incompatible with the highest exercise of free will.

The unsettling and irresistible thing about Miles for me was that I always had the sense that Miles chose me rather than the reverse. Miles always seemed to be waiting for me to join him; I was never waiting for Miles. This first struck me one spring morning in 2006, upon his return to school after a long absence. He had mistakenly come to school too early, not aware of our special schedule for the day. What shocked me was that he was sitting down and welcoming me to talk with him. Let me tell you this is quite a shocking experience for a head of school. This scenario played out again and again: Miles striding into the Oval for a football game, pushing through a great throng of students, a great moving knot of greeting. I saw this when he worked his way through the Dining Hall, moving from one table to the next, and finally making his way to the front table where the faculty sit. Here Miles sent out questions and thoughts to all assembled. Nobody moved faster than Miles did on our joyous Walking for Miles event. Even as weakness overtook him, Miles gave me the impression that he had invited me to his side, not the reverse.

Our feeling sad or sorry simply was not going to cut it for Miles. We had a responsibility to do better, perhaps first and foremost an obligation just to feel intensely. In his pulse seemed to beat the ee Cummings prayer, 'Please may I not pray for strength or beauty or wisdom, but may I pray only to be me.' This is what I took from Miles's appeal to us to shrug off 'survivor guilt' and take up 'survivor responsibility.' As Miles medical struggle grew increasingly savage, I seemed to see Miles become constant motion. Everywhere he seemed to invite us to love the unfinished and the unknown. As his plans beckoned to sushi, swing-dancing, glass-blowing, he seemed to say with Whitman, 'I contain multitudes.' Miles wrote seriously on several occasions about his intention to create a deep life or 'super-living' that nullifies time and his intention to load it so much more completely than our habits allow.

We loved Miles for what he brought to us, but as much for what he removed. Miles did not lightly enumerate the moments of great pride that he forfeited - college, marriage, children, grandchildren, retirement - but he asks us to understand what it is to embrace sacrifice. 'Life is not a tragedy, but tragedy is life,' Miles said. Only those who have tasted the bitterest of sacrifices can know the human extremities of character and courage."

As Charlie had been reading, the sound of the rain on the top of the tent began to increase in volume and intensity, necessitating that he raise his voice. Simultaneously, a long, heavy freight train that had been heard in the distance at the beginning of his eulogy had now come within 100 yards of us and, because the rain had softened the ground, we could actually feel the train through our feet. It was as if a great, unrestrained crescendo in a two year long opera had reached an enthralling climax. As Charlie reached the last paragraph of his eulogy there was a pelting rain, and a rolling train, and a shuddering terrain, and a shouting Shaw who said:

"Miles leads us to pose the question, 'what is the value of life without the great events of pleasure, plumage, and prestige?' Indeed, we ask, what is the value of life without Miles? For those of us brave enough to hear Miles, the only reality we can hold on to, and the final reality, is love, is kindness. It is our obligation to be as

alive and as wakeful as we can be, to reclaim those words that we have loaned out to the world for profit, those words that Miles offered so freely: courage, character, kindness."

I could imagine Miles looking on, thinking, "Yes, mission accomplished".

Wayne Alpern's Eulogy

As the train receded we stood there silently, wiping away tears. Miles' uncle, Wayne Alpern, a former lawyer and professional teacher of music composition had the sense of timing to wait in that stillness for our emotions to settle. Indeed even the rain, as if on cue, had become gentler. After a healthy pause Wayne took Charlie's place at the podium and said this to us, for us:

"Miles asked me to speak at his funeral. I told him it will be hard, but I would be honored to do that for him. I will tell you how I want to remember Miles, and how I think we should all remember him. I know in our weaker moments, like now, we are overwhelmed with grief at his loss. We feel sad for him and for us at his tragedy. But that is not how Miles lived. It's not how he confronted his own fate.

Miles was a powerful spirit. He lived with great courage. He called it 'superliving.' He didn't sulk, complain, or wallow in pity. He rose up. He never gave in, and never gave up. I want to be like Miles. I think we all do. I want to lift myself up and remember Miles the same way that he lived. If Miles could do that, so then must we.

Let me tell you how I will remember Miles. I remember a baby with a mischievous grin. I remember a boy running across a field with a quirky hop. I remember a kid who was always studying something no one else noticed. I remember a brother whose best friend was his sister. I remember a guy who was always a gentleman. And I remember a mind that was brilliant.

I remember an artist with delicate hands, a sculptor, and a writer who wrote astonishing things. I remember a visionary who dreamed dreams I didn't, and thought thoughts I couldn't. I remember a wizard on a computer, and a boy who became a man by saying no to death. I remember a giant who inspired others who suffered in need. And I remember a half million people reading his obituary the day he was buried.

I will remember Miles' stories and his imagination. I'll remember his choice of words, and the words he invented. I will remember his smile and his eyes. I will remember his handshake, and his curiosity. I will never forget those meteors. I remember a nephew who became my friend. I remember him thanking me for a pocketknife we both knew he would never use. I remember our meeting Johnny Damon, and climbing a castle on the Hudson. I'll remember his grace under pressure, and his final words to be kind. I'll remember his wisdom. And I will always remember Miles was not afraid.

That is the Miles I remember, and the Miles I urge you to keep in your heart. We can grieve he is gone, and Miles would too. But Miles would not mope. We all know he wouldn't want us to, and it would probably let him down. Miles was too vital, too compassionate, and much too kind. He would assure us not to worry, that it's OK. He would tell us to think and to feel, to learn and to grow from his own death. Above all, Miles asks each of us to wonder along with him, and yes, to be amazed.

And so, as we left behind gather here at his grave, and around the world, let us not measure our sorrow by his soul's precious worth. For then, our sorrow will surely have no end. Let us rather measure ourselves, and our own souls in accordance with his virtue. For then, the wonder of his life and the meaning of his death will thereby be assured.

Let us always remember what Miles gave, and not just what he lost. Let us cherish his existence, and not merely mourn his passing away. As we gently lower him down, let us begin to lift ourselves up. That is the Miles we know, and the Miles we love. And that is the Miles we are blessed to have shared, entrusted to remember, dedicated to honor—and the Miles I promised him I would speak about at the foot of his bed."

Wayne's eulogy was brilliant….a bull's-eye. He was the perfect uncle in Miles' life. They were very close. There was quiet tearfulness after Wayne's eulogy until we realized that we had impinged on the closing time of the cemetery and that the gravediggers were standing by to fill the grave. As is the Jewish custom, the mourners lined up at a wheelbarrow filled with soft dirt and, one by one, dropped a shovelful of dirt onto the top of the coffin. This was done with the tip of the shovel facing down rather than up to symbolize that death is the antithesis of life. Also, in order not to pass our grief to the next person, the shovel was not passed hand to hand but placed back in the dirt for the next person to take for himself. After we had performed this ritual we left the cemetery for our respective abodes. Nancy, Nina, and I returned to our house alone, as we had wished, leaving the remainder of the funeral party to its own devices until the time for evening prayers at our house, commencing seven days of mourning.

That evening on CNN, Anderson Cooper told his audience of Miles death, closing by saying, "Miles Levin was a friend of mine."

Public Condolences and Support

A steady trickle of mail began coming to us when it became clear Miles was on his way out. After the funeral, the mail brought a flood of cards and letters. Many people, aside from expressing their condolences, had included a check for the special non-profit fund that Nancy had created in Miles' honor. She established the fund in order to be able to help families dealing with pediatric cancer. The outpouring of donations was a testament to the sincere devotion of the CarePage readers. The fund received over $50,000 in donations within a month. One woman in the San Francisco area, who had no connection with our family, provided a gift of $10,000. But equally moving were the small donations accompanying heartfelt letters and cards. Here is one of my favorites which came from a Mr. Salvador Aguilar in San Francisco.

"August 16, 2007
Miles –
You don't know me, but I feel like I know you. You have touched my life in such a way that I cannot express with words. To read about your struggle with this disease and see through your words your courage and your profound view of life cannot be repaid, especially when that gift brought so much good to so many people like me. I see you like an angel that came to this world to show me the true meaning of the words kindness, courage, and respect. I will

never forget you and will always cherish this gift you have brought into my own life. I am able to see things in a different perspective thanks to you – how much we all should love ourselves and one another. Thank you. Salvador."

The Thanksgiving Day Ceremony

Friday, November 26, 2007

Because we had chosen to restrict the funeral to immediate family, we had denied our extended family, friends, and the CarePage community an opportunity to assemble and pay respects in person. We knew that some of them held sore feelings about this. So, to afford an opportunity to pay us a condolence call, Nancy and I devised a plan to hold a ceremony the day after Thanksgiving when many of Miles' classmates would be home from their first few months of the college experience. Because we expected hundreds of people, we asked Charlie Shaw if we could hold the ceremony on Cranbrook's football field, an area called the Oval. Charlie agreed, so we firmed up the particulars and then posted an invitation on CarePages and via e-mail.

The Friday after Thanksgiving was a crisp, clear day. Nancy had arranged for many gallons of fresh cider and donuts and hundreds of helium balloons to be delivered to the oval. Because the Cranbrook Educational Community was on holiday, Charlie Shaw and Jim Pickett set up a table and public address system on the playing field. That Charlie consented to the ceremony being held at Cranbrook and used his own holiday time to set up and attend the event demonstrates what a sincere and kind man is he. The event was called for 1:00pm. About 250 people had arrived by that time. Because there was a chill in the air, we suggested they stand in the sun alongside a brick wall facing the playing field. Charlie and Nancy made opening remarks of welcome and then the microphone was passed to me to state the following:

"One year ago this week, Miles Levin was starting what he believed would be his last round of chemotherapy. He was delighted and proud that he had endured and prevailed for 17 months of arduous, sickening treatment. On November 22, 2006 he wrote of an experience he had while driving from Beaumont Hospital to his classes at Cranbrook: 'The world was as bright and crisp as I could ever recall it being. I rolled down my window and stuck out my hand. The wind rushed cool through the seams of my fingers; sunshine warmed the back of my hand. Indian summer was heaving a last splendorous breath.' While driving he wrote the following with one hand on the steering wheel, 'I don't know what's in my future, relapse or cure....But if, God forbid, cancer cells do resurface, it's not going to be tomorrow, or next week - that much is pretty certain. I have time. And you can bet I'm savoring it.' He went on to say that the transformative power of cancer had been so beneficial to him that he might have volunteered for it if it didn't have such a mortality risk. And then, on Thanksgiving Day, 2006 he wrote that he was thankful:

— for the basic necessities that too many in this world do not have;

— for the luxuries which too often we take for granted;

— for family and friends and supporters worldwide;

— for kindness;

— for being alive, 'For this one I am thankful with all 100 trillion cells of my being'

He then wished his readers a happy Thanksgiving and health, peace, and fulfillment.

A few days later, on December 3rd, when he had completed what he thought would be his last round; he wrote 'I've played my hand as best I could. Now it's just a matter of waiting to see what cards the dealer holds. I hold my breath and enjoy the shapes of the clouds.'

Then, on December 9, he wrote: 'I cannot tell you how much I am enjoying life right now. This is it, friends, and right here.'

In the ensuing weeks, Miles dove head first into life, studying seven hours for the ACT exams, gearing up for the college application process, renewing his scuba diving certification, going to Disneyland and the Bahamas, volunteering at a warming shelter in Royal Oak, watching his hair grow back, and taking a full load of courses at Cranbrook. Miles was giving life a wholehearted embrace, a Miles hug.

And then, just ten weeks after going off treatment, the honeymoon was over. A recurrence was confirmed, and Miles quietly swallowed the bitterest pill of all, the acceptance of a terminal diagnosis. He wrote, on July 26 of this year, 'I'm getting quite a lesson in not getting what I want. Turns out it is one of the hardest we'll ever have to learn. I'm not a child anymore; I can't get away with throwing a tantrum. This is hard, and there's no easy way around that.'

His very last entry, on August 7, 2007 was as follows: 'I'm getting worse pretty quickly...All I can say is thank you. Thank you for your ongoing support of me and my family through this most difficult time.'

And so here are the gifts Miles gives us by example for this Thanksgiving: Grace under pressure, rejection of self-pity, ultimate acceptance of fate, expression of appreciation, and cultivation of a sense of gratitude. Clearly, he was a man, not a child. And we are sorry to have lost him. May he not only live in our memories, but in our lives."

Nancy then arranged for volunteers to pass out a balloon to everyone in attendance. When the balloons were released the wind carried them away very slowly in the most favorable direction for the crowd to continue to see them. They rose very gently and gradually and some people observed that they were in the shape of a giant letter "M".

If longevity is the mark of a good life, life was not good to Miles. On the other hand, as a Jewish sage once wrote, life's value lies not in whether life was good to you, but whether you were good to life. In Mile's grace, kindness, gratitude, sensitivity, and creativity we find that Miles was indeed good to life.

I recognize the truth in something written by Rabbi Morris Adler. Rabbi Adler was an esteemed theologian who was mortally shot by a deranged student in March, 1966, in front of 700 of his congregants. He wrote: "Our prayers are answered not when we are given what we ask, but when we are challenged to be what we can be." Miles Levin met this challenge.

Super Fans

Like any association of people, Miles' readers contained a wide variety of personalities who had a number of reasons for being Carepage readers. Some were lurkers who never commented. There were also those who were exceptionally devoted and generous of spirit. Among these (any there were many others) were:

- Dirk Baezner – Dirk, from the east coast of the US, would frequently contribute with warmth and supportive comments. Here is an example from July, 2007 when Miles was in New York "Just want you to know there is an invisible line outside the 'Miles in New York' theatre that makes everything else playing here look like a flop. If Miles is interested in more fun with friends, we're everywhere, lined up around the block, just for him. Just look for the guy sleeping in line for tickets. That's me ☺'

- Laura Berman, a Detroit News journalist, fought with her editors to cover Miles' story. They couldn't see the newsworthiness of another kid with cancer. Once published, her compassionate story led directly to coverage by CNN.

- Carol Costello, a CNN reporter who read Laura Berman's story and brought it to the attention of her producer, Rose Arce, who shepherded it through meetings at CNN which led to it being covered by Anderson Cooper's AC360 news show.

- Jacob Feord – Jacob was an eleven year old when he began reading and contributing to our Carepage. His expressiveness and innocence made him a favorite among the other readers. He organized a fundraising bake sale in our community which Miles attended, to Jacob's delight.

- Susan Fleming, a Florida attorney with whom we had no prior connection and who travelled to our house to pay her respects in person.

- Sasha Gerdej – a journalist in Ljubljana, Slovenia who was a constant source of internet hugs and warm thoughts. She created a special website devoted to Miles as her hero. She also travelled from Slovenia to our house to pay personal respects. A sensitive and warm soul, she eventually left journalism and devoted herself to assisting disabled individuals.

- Dave Gross, a Tiffin, Ohio paramedic who sent Miles Tiffin Fire and Rescue patches and paraphernalia and was a devoted CarePage reader and writer.

- John "Jonny" Immerman – John, a cancer survivor, was one of Miles' first supporters. We met through mutual friends. He had a special rapport with Miles and a very youthful and fresh way of saying things. He runs a Chicago based non-profit which pairs up cancer survivors with cancer patients across the US.

- Nancy Levin, Miles' mother, and his fan club president, tirelessly devoted her heart, soul, time, and intellect to see that no option went unconsidered, no resource unavailable, no hope undiminished, no comfort ungiven.

- Craig Mason – Craig, from Houston, was a self appointed guardian angel who was a frequent contributor and constant source of supportive, positive, remarks.

- The Medical Providers – Although the state of the medical arts did not allow for Miles' survival after the cancer had spread beyond the inception site, every effort was made to extend and enhance Miles' life. The medical team included dozens of unnamed but devoted pediatric floor nurses, as well as the following physicians: Leonard Wexler of Memorial Sloan Kettering Cancer Center; Charles Main, Peter Chen, Souheil Gebara, Ken Kernan, and doctors Morden and Bennett of the Beaumont Health Center; Corola Arndt of the Mayo Clinic; Gordon McLorie and Patricia LoRusso of the Detroit Medical Center Children's Hospital; Larry Baker of the University of Michigan; Peter Houghton of St. Judes; James Nachman of the University of Chicago;

Terry Fry of the National Institutes of Health, and many other physicians.

- Dave Nickason from Rochester, New York who was always posting encouraging comments and has continued to reach out and comfort us.

- Sylvia Pesek who drove all the way from Texas to pay her respects and who continues to send us white roses every year.

- Sally Read – Sally's comments always had great depth. She wrote that her participation on our Carepage evolved to the point where it became a commitment: "I don't know about anyone else, but I have taken a solemn oath and made a promise to stand guard, too….In many ways we are all 'mothering' Miles…..we are all in this together….it is a choice that passes all understanding

- Dianne Rice, a poet and writer who felt Miles' healing touch in reading his CarePage.

- Riki and Jerome Shaw were not only devoted to Miles but had the willingness and ability to be exceedingly helpful. Aside from being regular readers, they arranged and paid for two trips on private jets for Miles and Nancy to return from New York to Detroit. When Riki and Jerome learned that Miles and Nancy might be in New York City for a month they mailed a check to us for a very substantial sum with a note suggesting that we find something more comfortable than Ronald McDonald House. We framed the unused check as a symbol of their generosity.

We are grateful for every reader who helped give purpose to Miles journey, or as he called it, his "ugly blessing." Thank you all.

CPSIA information can be obtained at www.ICGtesting.com
Printed in the USA
BVOW030148101211

277943BV00006B/70/P